HEART WORK

19 Expressions of Heart-Centered Leaders

Glenn Thomas

This publication is designed to provide accurate and authoritative information in regard to the subject matter covered. It is sold with the understanding that neither the author nor the publisher is engaged in rendering legal, accounting, securities trading, or other professional services. If legal advice or other expert assistance is required, the services of a competent professional person should be sought.

From a Declaration of principles Jointly Adopted by a Committee of the American Bar Association and a Committee of Publishers and Associations.

Library of Congress Cataloging-in-Publication Data

Publisher: Heart Work Books & Publishing, LLC, 2020
support@glennathomas.com

Design by: ALYN, https://www.alynmarketinggroup.com

ISBN: 978-0-578-23359-8

10 9 8 7 6 5 4 3 2 1

Michelle,
Heart Work is the way;
keep on serving!
thank you;
Glenn

CONTENTS

Dear Leader...

As I write this letter (2020) our world is experiencing an unreal pandemic. The Coronavirus is ravaging the world, infecting millions and killing hundreds of thousands. This unknown disease has relegated our world to shelter-in-place and keep our physical distance as lives are upended and torn to pieces. There are few words to describe the shock and fear that people are feeling around the world, and America hasn't seen such tragedy since the 1918 flu pandemic.

And at the same time, America and the world is responding to an unrest towards the hundreds of years of systematic oppression and overt violence against Black lives in America. These moments are critical; these moments are empowering every human being to take a personal account of empathy, humanity, and dignity.

This book, this collection of learning experiences, has more meaning right now than I could have ever imagined. *Heart Work* is a symbol of the time, energy, and commitment that it takes for each of us to dig deep into our souls and discover who we truly are as God's children. And now this work speaks volumes to what we will begin to experience in the coming months and years. There are so many questions to ask. How will we cope? How will we recover? How will we move on? The answers are few right now, but we know for sure that the answers will include some intentional heart work.

I didn't begin writing this book with the thought of addressing a global pandemic and civil unrest. But here we are and the expressions found in this book are all too relevant for the times we are currently experiencing and will continue to recover from in the coming years. Yet, I stay encouraged by the humanity and courage of first responders, caretakers, neighbors, protesters, elected officials, and frontline workers through these seemingly dark and tumultuous times. And like America's beloved former First Lady Michelle Obama so eloquently stated, "Fear is not a proper motivator...hope wins out."

I am more than inspired by your willingness to be open to the possible. I was once in a place in life where I equated my happiness with how well my bank account looked, and how quickly my career progressed. All too often I privately expressed my outrage against oppression, violence, and injustices. If this hasn't been your experience, then I applaud you. But if you ever have had these moments, then I empathize with you.

My story is not who I am, but it has informed how I have grown. I write this letter to you to say just a few things: *1) I wish for you the peace and joy that every human being should experience in their lives, regardless of how prominent your worldly identity is defined. 2) I pray that you live your life from the inside-out, loving yourself so that you can selflessly love others; and 3) I challenge you to do your heart work, in your time, with all the commitment and grace that you have to give. The world needs each of us, more than ever before. Are you ready?*

Glenn Thomas

(My purpose statement posted on my home refrigerator - Glenn Thomas)

"The highest human act is to inspire." ~ **Ermias Asghedom**

For almost two years I have stepped in front of my refrigerator
and read this quote that I wrote for myself over four years
ago. I named it my purpose statement. It is the first thing I
see when I enter my kitchen and I see it at least ten times a
day, if not more. This book is a product of this quote. I
appreciate you reading this book; but more importantly, I am
grateful for how you will share and inspire others with the
information you take away from this book.

Be an inspiration. I love you.

DEDICATION

To my grandparents, parents, sister, aunt, friends, and mentors - I thank you for all that you have done and continue to do in my life. This book doesn't happen without you. Cheers to the heart work to come!

And to my heart and joy, Jennifer, Grayson, and Zoe. Nothing in the world comes before you, and nothing ever will...You three have taught me how to love, and I am forever changed because of you. I love you!

"Love transforms the lost into leaders, the hurt into healers, and the defeated into conquerors." - Glenn Thomas

INTRODUCTION

When I was younger, I dreamed of changing the world. Maybe you had a similar dream, maybe you didn't. But I never really knew specifically how I would change the world or what I would do to change the world. I just assumed that the world needed a little change based on my youthful lens. No matter if it was racial discrimination that I learned about in middle school or the HIV crisis that stunned me as a high schooler when I heard Magic Johnson retire from the NBA. I was just a forever optimist about contributing to the world something of value that would bring some level of goodness to people.

Over time, as I began to become an adult and more mature, I somehow started to be less of an optimist and more of a realist. Life, as I was learning, was revealing to me some harsh truths and stunning realities. Life could be unfair and people could be mean, and the dreams that you once were inspired by could be torn down in the blink of an eye by strangers and friends alike.

But over time, as I struggled with these truths, I began to reach deep into my faith and ask myself some tough questions. I was over being a "realist." I wanted more joy in my life, more optimism, and more belief in the goodness of the world, despite the negativity that I was seeing and hearing. The fact is the world is filled with all types of goodness and joy and people who care for each other. We choose what we see, how we interpret things, and how we feel. I wrote this book to share my lens of how *heart work* is the way we can individually and collectively present our narrative of what life reflects and how we ultimately discover the best in ourselves while inspiring the best in others.

I don't claim to be this super enlightened being. But what I have done in my life is to begin the journey of being honest with myself. I mean honest. Yes, I love the Lord, and yes I am imperfect. And yes I struggle daily to figure out things that challenge me in life. But what I don't do anymore is lie to myself, because I grew tired of making up excuses for why I wasn't being a good friend, or a present husband, or a more patient father. I was tired of being a high performing manager of things, and a poor servant to people. But for me to make a shift in my life I had some work to do. I didn't know what to call this work, other than I knew I had to get to work on me.

So between therapy and writing, taking personal time, and doing some honest deep reflection, I began to endeavor on a journey that would ultimately change me forever. I came to a place in my life that I wasn't going to sacrifice "me" for anything or anyone. Because a healthy, joyful, and grateful "me" was what God created me to be. This experience, this life journey was all about working inside my heart...not on my heart, but "inside" my heart. My *heart work* was (is) a process of me working on me from the inside-out...being purposeful, accountable and disciplined just enough to take the next step and the next step to reveal me.

I decided to write this book because it was a story that needed to be told - an authentic, imperfect story of a personal journey that has changed my life for the better. My prayer is that you will read something that speaks to you and your journey. If only one word, one line, or one story...whatever it is; I offer this book to you in hopes that my story inspires you to tell your story, so that we all are inspired to live our lives in greater gratitude, purpose, and love.

HEART WORK

Leading with Heart

The legendary Dr. Maya Angelou so eloquently once said, "I can be changed by what happens to me. But I refuse to be reduced by it." As I am writing this chapter, we are currently in the midst of a global crisis (COVID-19) and civil unrest in America, protesting and fighting against oppression and violence against Black lives; and I pray that we don't allow these moments to reduce us; rather, I challenge all of us to use it to strengthen us. And like so many times in our lives, when we are forced to face a challenge that emotionally and mentally tests us, we have to be prepared to not only face the challenge but also to overcome it.

Over the past twenty years, I have had the privilege of serving in leadership roles for government agencies, nonprofits, and even a Fortune 500 company. And having served in roles that challenged me personally and professionally, the one thing that stuck with me the most is that no matter what one does professionally, how well you treat people - how well you serve people, should always be your highest priority.

No matter if I was serving on boards, interviewing leaders on my podcast, or spending time with my family, I came to understand that the keys to living my best life were not rooted in just committing to hard work. I realized that the aha moments - those transformational revelations, came in the most difficult and challenging times in my life; when I dared to be vulnerable, courageous, and strong enough to do the necessary *heart work* that is ever so elusive in so many of our lives.

You may ask, "How does this apply to me and the people I serve?" In the past, each and everyday people would leave their homes and go to work with every single piece of joy or pain they were experiencing in their lives. And because so many organizations lacked psychologically safe cultures, leaders would often fall short of helping their teams reveal their inherent greatness. That was our reality. But now our new reality will require that we don't make those same mistakes. The old, traditional professional development experiences just won't suffice anymore, not now, and not for our new norms.

There is nothing status quo about the times we are living in now; and there is nothing standard about the collection of learning experiences in this book. The future of work is uncertain for all of us. And how we unify around our new normal will undoubtedly be one of our most ambitious endeavors in the coming years. When I founded Leadership Matters Group in 2013, I had one goal in mind: to inspire leaders to lead with love. Yes, I know; a little different, not the normal business strategy, and maybe even a little ambitious.

But after demonstrating to organizations just how leading with love - doing their *heart work* makes a clear impact, it began to make sense. It began to make a difference in the lives of their teams. At the core of all of what we do as leaders is *heart work*: leading, teaching, inspiring, empowering, executing...it is all *heart work*. So when challenges present themselves, will your team be prepared?

Are you ready to support your teams and their needs as you construct strategies to engage with teammates? What should they expect from you? What conversations are you going to have? What safe spaces will be created for teammates to just be themselves?

Heart Work answers these questions and so many more. This book was designed to challenge leaders with relevant and relatable questions, to guide open and transparent discussions, and to examine the application of ideas and strategies. And through it all, ensuring that each learning experience is guided through the heart. This book covers the 19 transformative attributes of heart-centered leaders; expressions that address our *Heart, Mind, Wellness, and Leadership*. *Heart Work* is a personal growth experience that challenges leaders to be introspective, curious, thoughtful, and deliberate.

This content and the learning experience was created specifically for the person you are and the challenges you encounter in life; and the dreams and hopes you envision for yourself, your family, and your future. *Heart Work* focuses on you (the leader) so you can be all that you were created to be. We know that when you can be your best self, your leadership, your team, and the organizations you serve, begin to win at unimaginable heights.

BEFORE YOU BEGIN

In the space below, write down "why" you want to read this book...after you are finished reading or when you feel moved to do so, come back to this page and revisit what you wrote.

How do you feel now after reading this book? What thoughts immediately come to mind? Continue to process why you decided to read this book and share with others what "heart work" means to you.

_____

_____

_____

_____

_____

_____

_____

1

PRESENCE

I A healing space I

Healing in a state of presence is where we must begin to work through what troubles our hearts.

. . . .

As I stood there crying and sobbing with such intensity that I couldn't breathe, I felt the weight of the world on me - and he tried his best to comfort me. My mother in the background said little. He attempted to say more - but it was not enough. It would prove to never be enough. He left walking right out of the door as if I was nothing. I could see his mouth moving, saying words to calm me, but I couldn't hear a sound. My heart felt as if it were in my stomach, traveling at lightning speed to the floor.

There was nothing to hope for in that moment. Who knew a five-year-old could feel that complex, stirring, jolting level of emotion? As the door slammed shut, the silence was deafening. Life at that moment shifted and time stood still. I needed someone to do something. But there was nothing. Silence. No words. And I was there, tears and all, by myself in a world of emptiness. My dad had effectively walked away from us, from me, just that quick.

The separation for whatever it was worth was probably a good thing. I have never known the true story of what happened and to this day it seems that whatever it was, my parents have little to say about it. But for sure, what did happen affected me forever. I never knew just how their separation had impacted my life until it was clear to me that I had emotional scars that I couldn't diagnose. It was painful. At the age of two, my mother moved our family to Atlanta from Los Angeles. Of course, being two, I couldn't recall or understand the magnitude of the situation. And God knows I am glad that those memories don't exist for me.

I remember staying with my aunt for a while when we first moved back to Atlanta. It was cool. My fondest memories were centered around just playing in the yard and not having any cares in the world. We were a typical family. I had grandparents and cousins, and soon some friends in the neighborhood. My dad not being there really never mattered until that faithful day he walked out. That's the day that I first understood that he didn't live with us and was leaving to go back to Los Angeles - his home.

I was five when he walked out of that door. That day would be the beginning of countless moments of him walking out of the door back to his home, leaving us by ourselves. "Why are you leaving?", I asked. It was more like screaming and begging. But it was much of the same story. It was always time for him to get back to work. And he would always drive, he never flew. As long as I've known my dad he has never flown in an airplane; something about being an airplane mechanic in the service and not trusting planes. So he always would drive a van or his motorhome to Atlanta. And a couple of times he took me to visit his parents in Mississippi to spend time on the family farm. My recollections of those days are refreshing. We would ride our three-wheelers and play baseball in the field. We even had motorcycles and ate watermelon while throwing the rinds to the cows. As a kid, that was living. I cherished those days and moments that I spent with him. They were few and far in between, but they mattered.

On a couple of occasions, my mom put me on a plane to visit my dad in Los Angeles. I would help out at the car lot my dad owned. I made a mean pot of coffee and I was eager to always help. That pot stayed fresh and full to the rim; if you happened to be in LA during that time, you would have wanted to drop by. You missed out on an awesome cup of hot, strongly brewed cup of joe.

But he did have to work so I spent quality time with his assistant and she kept me busy. She would take me to swimming lessons in Beverly Hills, which I thought was pretty awesome. And afterward, she would stop by the most amazing restaurant that any child has ever had the pleasure of dining at - Taco Bell. That Taco Bell was the best back in the day. I made sure to grab the Mexican pizza, two burrito supremes (no sour cream), and a handful of tacos...it depended on how hungry I was. Those times were what they were. I had accepted that he lived there and I lived with my mom. But as time passed I realized that he wasn't moving to where I was, so I wanted to move there. My mother had plenty to say about that but she didn't close the door fully shut to the idea.

My dad and I had come to an agreement. I would move to LA for high school and attend a nice school near the beach in Marina Del Rey. I was excited, but the plan was abandoned for what my dad thought was a better plan. He decided that I would walk to school and attend the school two blocks up from his house. Now, for all of you who don't know much about LA and the neighborhoods, this may seem crazy, but listen closely because I need to educate you on what was happening in some LA neighborhoods in 1991...it was rough; the Rodney King verdict riots had recently happened, and the movie *Boyz n the Hood* was very real to me; and my dad lived off of Crenshaw and Slauson...so, let's just say, the realist in me was not pleased with the options I had.

Seriously, it was tough back then. A couple of years earlier my cousin had been gunned down on our street right in front of our other cousin; right in front of his own home. And though the gang-banging had subsided to some degree, there was still a climate of violence in certain neighborhoods and schools. And my dad's neighborhood school was one that I just didn't want to chance my life with. I couldn't understand for the life of me why my dad wouldn't keep his word and send me to a safer school. It was another turning point for me; I looked at him differently, still not fully understanding my emotions, but knowing that I wasn't feeling the love like I thought I should. Maybe I was making more of the situation than it was, but I didn't know any other way to look at it. After middle school, I wouldn't visit LA for another three years. And even that visit wasn't to see my dad. He found a way to visit me while I was there but the relationship has never been the same.

I was a fighter growing up, a modern-day UFC ultra-ultra lightweight. I wasn't big enough to be anyone's bully, but I know that I can safely say that I had the infamous teenager "anger issues" syndrome. I was mostly a happy kid, but I had an angry heart. It was well disguised, but I was hurting and you would have never known just how hurt I was. I lived what most people would call a fairly uneventful upbringing. I really can't tell a story of great tragedy or misfortune; just occasional bumps in the road that touches all of us. I was just in a normal family; a middle-class neighborhood with pretty good friends, and some great adult influences. So why in the hell was I so hurt inside? I eventually figured out that I was actually just human. Yep, even in my normal upbringing, I had a whole lot of stuff inside of me that was hurting - go figure, like most teenagers in the world, I was growing up.

As far back as I can remember my mom kept me busy. Pee-wee football at five (that ended after the first game when some kid had the unfortunate pleasure of getting rampaged on the field). That had to be the quickest football career in the history of humankind. But I had baseball, and it served me well for a while. I loved baseball and my mom knew just how to bribe my obedience with threats of missing practice, or God forbid an actual game.

Having something to always do as a kid was a great way to stay busy and active. And adults do the same thing; staying busy can be healthy and unhealthy. The challenge for many of us is that we engage in distractions, or activities, that can be harmful and dangerous to our mind and body. After experiencing the ups and downs of my "distractions" for a great part of my early adulthood, I found that being present with what is in front of me is far healthier than escaping to something that can harm me. More than ever, I feel as though *presence* is what the world needs to experience most.

Like most southern families church was at the center of my house as a youngster. Church choir, church bell ensemble, church acolytes, church usher...you get the point, right? We were heavily involved in our church, everything you can imagine and more. It was weird though. We went to church but my mom could snap at us like a drill sergeant and punish us like someone had stolen her Gucci bag (in fairness, I don't recall her ever having a Gucci bag). But God only knows, LOL. I stayed super busy and because of that I think that the hurt inside of me stayed inside of me; and unfortunately for the worse. It didn't start to rear it's head until I became a little older, right about the time the hormones starting kicking in around middle school.

That's what happens when we don't take the time to be present in the moments that are critically important to us. It gets worse. We can't escape those moments, we are just repressing them in that decision to *not be present* in them. The most damaging behavior that we exhibit towards ourselves is the act of covering up our hurt and trauma. It lingers, festers in our spirit, and rests in the deepest and darkest corners of our being. Yet, there is no escaping or getting rid of pain that we never experience presence with; the resolve comes when we decide to acknowledge the pain, and deal with our truth.

In middle school, I played trumpet in the band, was in "gifted class" (not sure why sometimes), and had an after-school job in the school store. It was a life that by most accounts was pretty cool. I was into girls, friends, and fun. And in that order. This is also during the time that my dad visits were becoming more scarce and I began to consciously notice it. But I still had my friends and stayed busy so much that I pushed those feelings aside the best I could. Eventually, what was once a pronounced emotional pain had become distant anger.

At home, life was interesting, my mother was a school teacher and my sister was five years my elder so we were never really what I would define as friends. The relationship between my mother and sister however was indeed the thorn in my side and I watched how they would interact to my dismay. Look, my mom wasn't any different from most parents back then I don't think. I just couldn't understand their relationship and the dynamic between mother and daughter. It was what it was and I saw what I saw...but never in a million years did I think those moments in time would have a lasting effect on me, on my life that was to become.

Throughout middle and high school I was a pretty decent student and kept my nose clean for the most part. I did what kids did back then; started drinking at age thirteen because my friends had older siblings, my mom had liquor in the house, and you know the line...one plus one equals two. So there you have it, drinking and drugs at a very early age in life. I know, a crazy sequence, but it was my reality and it was my distraction. Nevertheless, while I was growing up, my mind was growing, my emotions were intensifying and my relationship with both my mom and dad had become strained for totally different reasons.

Hurt in our human body manifests in a variety of ways. Many times we literally can't discern whether we are hurt or just angry. Sometimes we are both. I was both for a long time. But being angry when you are young, coupled with all the other crap that is happening in your life, can be and mostly is a recipe for total disaster. I thought that I was experiencing the normal teenage stuff, but my aunt knew there was something deeper happening. She should have known, hell, she was a trained school counselor. She worked with kids all the time. She would constantly tell us, in her most calm and thoughtful voice, "Y'all need some counseling." And I remember those words like it happened yesterday...and now that I think about it, it probably did happen yesterday, LOL - considering that my mom and I are still "working" on our relationship, counseling wouldn't be a horrible idea but I digress.

As a kid, we never did receive counseling. My sister moved out of the house into a college dorm and we continued on this journey of *who had more power in the house.* I will admit that I lost that war and most of the battles that came along with it. But the experiences of growing up all came to a boiling point. And hence began the period where my hurt starting hurting others.

In high school, I decided to wear out my welcome at home and become what *old school* folk call "slick talkers." My mom and I bumped heads on more than one occasion and my feelings were like any teen, but it was deeper. We had struggles that just weren't normal to me (admittedly, I had no clue what normal was) and I was in a place of rebellion and disdain that I know hurt her and without a doubt hurt me. From stealing her car and wrecking it at the bank drive-thru, to staying out so late that I had to make up entire incidents that never happened, I was acting out and not caring about anything but getting out of Atlanta. So I headed as far north as I could without landing in the snow; I ended up in Durham, North Carolina.

In my early college days, my dad was given a life-threatening health diagnosis. By this time, after disappointment after disappointment, I wasn't even clear on what I should do. Should I be there for him while he began going through this process of healing when he couldn't even seem to be there for me when I needed him? Honestly, that question wasn't even really necessary. On the inside, I was scared for him, but on the outside, I kept moving on with my life. Maybe he didn't need me or didn't care if I was there. But whatever the circumstances were, he never mentioned it and neither did I. At that moment I just didn't want to be present. I knew the right thing to do was to be there for him, but my pride, my anger, my hurt, just would not allow my head to tell my heart to do the right thing. My pain had turned to spite. Those were days I can never get back and I hurt myself more than anyone else. You see, hurt people have difficulties seeing through the fog of their pain. I couldn't see clearly. Though I was hurt, I was operating my life on crutches of excuses, self-pity, and anger.

And so my hurt became the way I lived; processing and thinking every single day about the past, and drowning out the hurt with anything available to me. Throughout my college experience I had a great time; a brief stint with the marching band, then two years on the tennis team, and a pledge experience that landed me the line name *Perseverance* in the brotherhood of Omega Psi Phi Fraternity, Inc. I couldn't have asked for a better time. But the hurt was always there, and it showed up and showed out in the worst of times.

Needless to say, alcohol was plentiful in college. And drinking coupled with girls and eighteen-year-old freedom can be a toxic cocktail, especially when you stir it with deep emotional anguish. Maybe I had a little too much fun at the expense of trying to let loose; maybe I had a little too much of everything that life had to offer. But what was real for me was that I was trying to do all those things without addressing the one thing that I couldn't see my way clear to address - my pain.

Social scientist and author Brené Brown is famous for saying "Hurt people, hurt people." And when I first heard her say those words I believed I was fairly self-aware. But it hit me like a ton of bricks and I felt like I was time traveling back in my mind to all the people I had hurt. The words I may have used or didn't use; the times I wasn't present or just didn't care enough to let someone know that I loved them and appreciated them. That was me. Not a total jerk but a jerk nonetheless.

Getting through college was a blur. I took the five-year plan because I was cooking in my own personal kitchen of life and mayhem. And my student loan debt is reflective of these horrible decisions I made. I was involved with so much, yet I was searching for something very specific. I was seeking a connection in things and people. I threw myself into pledging my fraternity because it was something that I had always wanted to do since I was in middle school; primarily because I couldn't imagine being anything other than an Omega, but also because one of the few men in my life was an Omega man. And he was sharp, he was cool, worked hard, cared for his family, and he stood tall. I respected that; I appreciated that.

I recall one time as I sat at my dining room table in my apartment, and he shared some words of wisdom with me that I have never forgotten. He said, "Sparky, (that's my nickname) when you become an Omega, go to work, do your job, and let people call on you. A man that works hard need not raise his hand for selection, he will be selected by the demonstration of how hard he works." Those words stuck. And I have tried to live by them all of my life.

During my final years of college at the illustrious NC Central University, I began attending church more. Many of the local area college students attended a pretty popular church named Orange Grove Missionary Baptist Church. I grew up in the church, but church was different for me by the time I arrived at college. I had experienced so much. And the pain I brought with me to college began to manifest in everything I was involved in; girlfriends, school, health, you name it, I needed something else. I needed God.

As I stood in Orange Grove one day, the sermon was powerful, the music was moving, and I was in a place of depletion. I had to surrender the hurt, the pain, the anger, the fear, the feelings of depression. I was in my moment of holy worship. The next thing I knew I was standing up, crying, with my hands raised in the air, surrendering it all because I had nothing left in my being to fight anymore. I needed Him. And He knew it and I knew it. It was a moment in time that I will never forget. I knew things would be different from then on and I knew that meant that I would have to be different. I would have to choose to let God love me and begin to love myself enough to begin healing. What I didn't know at the time was that the process of healing would take far longer than I could have ever imagined.

I was in the process of getting emotionally stronger. I had always been able to compartmentalize most things in my life but this was a time to begin opening up. It was difficult and not as easy as I thought it would be. But I was aware and that was a start. I was aware of the hurt I was feeling, had been feeling, and began to acknowledge that I had some work to do on *me*. The journey started with great intention and challenged me every step of the way. I recall getting close to graduating from undergrad and having nightmares that I wouldn't be able to attain my degree. It was literally touch and go, down to the last credit. God only knows that I prayed harder than I had ever prayed for anything in my life. I had realized that I needed to do whatever it took to get across that stage. At the same time, I was having an internal struggle about what I would do with my lowly 2.3 GPA in history (it probably was lower), and several failed LSAT attempts on my resume (I tried, God knows I did).

So I turned to the one thing that I had any interest in - public sector management. I know, it sounds boring. But I always had an interest in the way history shapes our culture, how government shapes our policies, and the way public servants help to influence our lives. But before I could get to this newfound career I needed some qualifications. I figured a degree in public administration wouldn't hurt. But it would take more than an act of God to get me into graduate school. Considering that my undergrad GPA was well below acceptable levels and my entrance exam was unsurprisingly shameful, I needed a miracle of all miracles.

So I did what I did best, I pulled together the right decision-makers and made a big ask. It was a tough sell but in the end, the graduate school reps decided to allow me entrance on probation. I am pretty sure they figured I would eventually drop out like a dehydrated marathon runner. But I had other plans. I knew that if I used just a little of my God-given common sense, I could get through this program. So I changed my attitude and started focusing on what mattered - my education.

Four years later, in a two-year program, I was a graduate. I had experienced so much. A tumultuous personal relationship with a girl, a summer overseas in a graduate assistantship program that I made a "C" in (it was worth every penny), and a defining moment that helped me start a non-profit for kids with challenging backgrounds. These four years had God written all over them. My hurt, my joy, and everything in between happened in those four years. I was getting better - but still not where I wanted to be. Little did I know that those four years would look like the kiddy ride at the mall compared to what would happen next.

Ever since I was a kid I enjoyed traveling. I think it was those few trips that I had with my dad traveling across the country back and forth from Los Angeles to Atlanta. I still love traveling to this day. And in my second year of graduate school, I had an opportunity to attend the Syracuse University study abroad graduate assistantship program based in Geneva, Switzerland. I say this to you with all of my being...*It changed my life.* If you have traveled overseas, you can relate; and if you have ever lived overseas for any meaningful length of time, then you definitely can relate.

I was assigned to work at the World Health Organization (WHO). It was 2001 and I thought this was the best thing ever. I was supporting the team that was completing the development of the first-ever World Mental Health Atlas. Part of my assignment was to transcribe the Spanish speaking regions content into English. But the most important thing I did while at WHO, was of course - travel! I traveled too much I'm sure. Friday's seemed to always be the start of a weekend of adventure.

Trains, planes, and automobiles - that was my motto. You name the western European country, I traveled there. I even ran into the queen of queens...no, not Queen Elizabeth...Queen Tina Turner! Yeah, I met (the loose definition of met) Tina Turner in Monaco. That was an amazing time. And yes, I know what you are thinking. And the answer is yes, she looked amazing! From the French Riviera to Barcelona, to Zurich and Rome, I loved all of my experience traveling and learning.

I ate the best food, danced at some of the best clubs, met some amazing people, and drank more than my liver could have ever imagined was humanly possible. And I drank, and drank, and drank. And my hurt was deep in those bottles as usual. My mother came to visit me towards the end of my stay in Geneva. We spent time together that seemed unlikely considering our relationship, but I welcomed it. We visited the Montreux Jazz Festival, traveled to France and ate Moroccan food, and just chilled. And on her last night there, my last week, I got so drunk that I couldn't remember how I made it back to the dorm. I embarrassed myself, my mom, and my cohort because I was sloppy drunk. I woke up the next day with a hangover from hell and ashamed. At the time, I didn't see what was going on, but it was all rooted in pain. It (drinking) always was.

From the time I was thirteen, I was a drinker. It didn't matter what it was, I would drink it. I chose to do it, I chose to abuse it, I chose to drown my pain in it. The only problem was the more I drank, the more I tried not to be present and the pain intensified. Nevertheless, I found myself in Europe drinking uncontrollably. These moments where I was conscious of what was happening but not able to process why it was happening, kept on happening. I went to Geneva to learn, have fun, and travel. I did all those things, just with the constant escapism into more harmful behavior. Not experiencing presence earlier in my life, in those moments that mattered in my life, was rearing ugliness in me that I could not bring myself to admit.

Healing in a state of presence is where we must begin to work through what troubles our hearts. And it takes sacrifice and a strong will to decide to be present; to not make excuses and to acknowledge and accept what has transpired in our lives, while asking one very important question - what can I learn? When we ask this question we are beginning to take a step forward towards *envisioning how we grow in our life-journey. This is the power of being present, being conscious of all that is happening with us, and allowing ourselves to experience it - all of it. Presence is a blessing of experiences, wrapped inside a gift of learning.*

I presence

Expression #1: If you believe you can run away from the painful things that haunt you, you are sadly mistaken. I've tried it, others have tried it, and I'm sure you have probably tried it. And I'm 100% sure that it hasn't worked for anyone. Take into consideration COVID-19 (the 2020 pandemic); if you weren't forced to be present, then you weren't paying attention. There has never been a time in recent history where being present in the moment has been more critical than during COVID-19. Are you present with your thoughts now? How about with your children or significant other? Or have you had the opportunity to be present in your faith? Either way, experiencing presence (in pain or pleasure) is powerful. Presence is where we must begin our journey to start our *heart work* so that we can do the necessary work of feeling, healing, and living.

Presence can be defined as the act of being consciously aware in a moment or circumstance. As children, when we were hurt physically or emotionally, our parents would tell us to try and get over the pain and dust ourselves off. It is how we were programmed growing up. In school, on the playground, at home, or wherever we were, as children we were always pushed to let things go and to not dwell on the bad things that happened to us in life. Conversely, some of us (myself included) tend to not be present even in the most joyous moments in our lives. Either we don't believe we deserve to be happy, or we feel less than or unworthy of goodness.

In many of us, there exists a natural desire to shy away from being present. We use outlets to get us through life's most difficult times. We turn to these outlets, that are best described as distractions: jobs, food, alcohol, sex, drugs, social media, television. They all are fairly normal aspects of life (some more than others) until we use them in a way to distract us from what's happening in our lives. They are mis-used in order to help us become less present in moments that we have labeled too difficult to face. We lean into them with ease because they bring us comfort and solace. We create stories in our minds that tell us if we just distract ourselves, we will forget all that is troubling us. Don't get me wrong, blowing off some steam with distractions isn't a totally bad thing - until we engage in them under the most unhealthy conditions.

But these distractions are not helping us. They are creating a false sense of security in our subconscious and allowing us to live life without addressing the real issues we are struggling with. What happens to that hurt, that issue that we just don't want to deal with? No, it doesn't go anywhere. It's not drowned out forever just by abusing your distraction. It stays right where it is and it does only one thing; it grows inside of you. In Pema Chodron's *Welcoming the Unwelcome*, she asks the reader to think about this - when life becomes complex, ask yourself, "Does *it* matter?" Answer the following question for yourself: How present are you in the moments of your life that matter?

Presence Exercise

This exercise is about reflecting, examining, and envisioning. There are several obstacles that hinder us from being present in the moments that matter. But, if we can focus and isolate the root cause(s), we give ourselves a greater chance of developing healthier behaviors.

Instructions: Answer the following questions for yourself in the notes section.

Q1: What makes you hurt or sad; excited or happy?

Q2: What are you fearful of in life?

Q3: What aren't you able to deal with?

Q4: Do you celebrate good things that happen to you?

Q5: Do you take time to feel the troubling things that are happening in your life?

Q6: Do you feel, "Presence" in your life?

Q7: How present are you in the low and high moments of your life?

Q8: Do these moments matter to you when they do occur? Are you present in them? If not, what stops you from being fully present in these moments that matter to you? If so, how do you exhibit presence?

Q9: *Do you believe in the statement, control what you can control? Are you controlling your state of presence in your life?*

After spending time with your responses, affirm for yourself how you would like to respond to being more present in moments that matter to you? Complete the following statement in the notes section:

"I want to show up and be present in the moments that matter by _____(fill in the blank)."

NOTES:

_____

_____

_____

_____

_____

_____

_____

2

RESILIENCE

I Get in the game I

When we are resilient...life will undoubtedly present us with the pay-off that can be even more rewarding than we initially envisioned.

I walked into my office, looked around, and said to myself, "I made it!" It was a rare moment of excitement for me. Not often did I exclaim so much joy, but I felt as though that moment was worthy of a night out with the fellas. I had recently been offered a job in a local government organization and I was on cloud nine. It was the same job that I had applied for while in graduate school and I was denied an interview twice; it was now my new job.

During my last year of graduate school, after closing down the nonprofit I started years earlier, I focused on landing a government job in enterprise management. I saw some postings in Charlotte, NC and I was intrigued. Early in my college years, I had a roommate from Charlotte. I had joined him on some trips home and I liked Charlotte, so it seemed like a great opportunity to move to a big city without the big city hustle.

I applied for a few jobs and got nowhere. There was one job as a management analyst that I wanted. But they never gave me a callback. I wasn't ready to give up on that job, so I had to find a way to get connected to the hiring department. This is what happened - I did what all blue-blooded, in a jam, tenacious, ambitious people do. I phoned a friend. And not just any friend; my frat brother who I had met just a couple of years prior. I asked him if he knew anyone that worked at the county manager's office, and to my surprise he did. Not only did he know someone, he knew thee one - the county manager. I was shocked, to say the least, but I knew that just because he knew him it didn't mean this road would be any easier.

But what it did mean was, at a minimum, I could probably get a meeting. All I wanted was 30 minutes of his time. The crazy thing was I didn't know exactly what I wanted. I knew that he couldn't, nor should he, just give me a job. So I asked my friend to put in a call to his friend and mentor and just let him know that I wasn't crazy and I wouldn't waste his time. My friend agreed but also was adamant that I would have to speak for myself and let the county manager know what I wanted and why I wanted it.

Before I knew it, I was sitting in the waiting area of the county manager's office, my plan in my head and my stomach on the floor. This was the county manager of the second-largest county in the state. I was a fourth-year graduate student who was sleeping in his friend's basement. I had to get it together, shake off the nerves, and step up like a champ. It was game time. I had my plan, my request, and I wouldn't turn away without it.

When you want something out of life you have two choices - go get it or quit. That's it - period. There is no magic remedy or secret strategy that will magically happen for your dreams to come true. Resilient people, hungry leaders, are going to achieve their goals because they understand that the word "no" only applies to those who don't want it.

As I sat down in his office, I vaguely remembered why I initially had asked for the meeting. But before I knew it I had gone into full-blown plan mode. I asked him if I could come intern for his office, for free, for four months. I figured if I could intern there while I was finishing my final semester in grad school, I could convince them to hire me for the same job that they hadn't even considered to interview me for.

Surprisingly, he agreed to let me intern, but then stopped me in my tracks and asked me, "Didn't you want to know how I got to be county manager?" I paused in embarrassment. I did want to know but I had forgotten that because I was so nervous. But he graciously shared with me his story and it was worth the experience. Though I was listening, I was still swimming in that moment; here was an opportunity for me to prove myself. And then, in that office, I realized that my life just got real - real fast. I was about to be working forty hours a week, attending graduate school at night back in Durham, and making no money. What the hell was I thinking? But again, hungry people always find a way to eat; and I was hungry!

As the county manager ended our conversation and escorted me to his colleague's office, I knew at that moment I was on a journey that would shape my life in ways I only had dreamed of. So many things went through my head. What if I failed? What if they didn't think highly of me? What if I ended up unemployed at the end of the internship? And then the next level of questions started to creep into my head. What if I can't afford to buy food, have a roof over my head, put gas in my car? (I ran out of gas twice, that's no fun.) I could just hear my mom saying, "Son, this is a bad idea." But the reality was, I didn't have any other options. This had to work. I had to knock this one out of the park.

After three months into my internship, I was at the point of completing my last semester. However, the kicker was, I had to take my comprehensive exams to graduate. The real kicker was that I only could take the exam three times, and I was on take three (talking about a stressful situation). I was falling to pieces, to say the least. So my internship supervisor and I agreed that I would take the fourth month of internship to study for the exam. I had passed two already so I only had to study for one question. The only problem was, it was in quantitative analysis - a class that I had taken three times and dropped twice. Let's just say, I wasn't fond of quantitative analysis...but who is?

The team sent me off with a great thank you party and I felt that the least I could do was to study for the exam and hit a home run. I was nervous, stressed, and scared. Life was getting real. The comprehensive exam was a tale of legend at NC Central University. There had been enough casualties of war who hadn't been able to pass by the third attempt...we call them the "lost clan" - basically, because they completed the program but couldn't graduate. Was it fair? Hell no. Did I want that distinction? HELL NO!

I was allowed to bring notes to the exam but that didn't calm my nerves. I drove to Durham from Charlotte the night before the test. As I sat in Chili's, a fine dining experience, of course, I prayed that the one question test would prove to be a question that I could answer just enough to get through. And to add pressure to the atmosphere, that internship that I had just completed would turn into a full-time job if I could just answer this one question correctly.

That night I didn't get much sleep. I was thinking about the what-ifs and pondering a future I couldn't set my sight on, because I had to answer one question to set my life in one direction. Without answering that one question correctly I couldn't receive my graduate degree. And that degree was a requirement to land that full-time job. I could have easily folded. So much was riding on this test. I had done and sacrificed so much to get to this point in my life. But the truth of the matter was that I had only skimmed the surface. There was far more to do and I needed to get my head in the game and finish the job. The fact is, when you stay in the game after all the rejection and failure, you will always have a chance.

On the day of the test, I was fried. As in tired as hell, nervous, shook. All the emotions that I normally never had, I was having them in that moment. I entered the room and sat down. There in that room sat actual lost clan members who, at the time, didn't know (I didn't know either) that they would become part of the lost clan. I breathed calmly, I think, waiting for the test question to come to my desk. There was no time limit, but there need not be one. The way this test was written, you either knew how to answer the question or you didn't. And if you didn't know, you could sit there for a year, with multiple books, and you would still fail.

The test landed on my desk like a sack of rocks. It felt like the world had just stopped and I had to save it with my one answer. As I turned the sheet over to read the question, out of the corner of my eye I noticed familiar words, and thought to myself...this...may...be...it...it was, it was the same question that we had studied in a previous class. I had worked on it for days alongside my professor; solving that problem was the highlight of one of the many study sessions we had. And it was right there in my notes. I haven't ever in my life felt relief like that. My life as I knew it began in that moment (at least that's what I thought).

Now, graduation was imminent. I received a call from my internship supervisor and it was great news. They would be sending me a formal job offer (I still have the original letter). I had fought for that job, sacrificed for that job, and the moment was right there. I had achieved something that so many told me was a misguided attempt in futility.

In the backdrop, I was having fun celebrating and signing a new lease for an uptown Charlotte apartment close to all the action. And yes, I was drinking like prohibition was on the next legislative bill in Congress. I was living the life of a man who had escaped a life of the lost clan (no shade). My new job's direct deposit hit at 12:45 am Thursday, so that meant that Wednesday night was party night. And I mean every Wednesday night was party night. Shots, beers, liquor, whatever the bartender was making we were drinking and it didn't matter when they closed because we could just keep the party going at someone else's house.

The only downside was when the alcohol got the best of me. When the night turned ugly and my car ended up in a tow lot, and my boss had to come to pick me up from my house - that's when a good thing turned really bad. I thought that I was doing well; that I had come through those early life pains and hurt. But in reality, I was living a complex existence. I could see the trajectory of what had taken place in such a short period of time: I came, I thought I conquered, and I definitely collapsed. And it was all fueled by my need to escape.

It was the budget season and all hands were on deck. Aside from my nightly affairs and excursions, the expectation was that I would do my job when it came to working. And I prided myself to live by this mantra. Our team had been engulfed in reconciling positions for each county department. If you are wondering what that entails, just imagine a stack of perforated sheets that have anywhere from hundreds to thousands of positions with names attached to them. Reconciling them means you must make sure that they are valid positions that can be added to the new budget tally.

I was handed a task to have my reconciliations completed by a certain time and was overwhelmed by this exercise. I had reconciled positions before, but not to this degree. So I gave it the champions try and headed off to do my job. About halfway through I realized something; this was tedious as hell! It seemed pretty straight-forward, go by each line and verify that every position was accurate.

The only problem was, this was taking far longer than I imagined it would. So what did I do? I took a short cut and failed to thoroughly do my job. And yes, my supervisor caught the errors in my work. He was so disappointed; but he calmly let me know, "This is what we have to do; be thorough." And he was right, I needed to grow up and begin to take my work more seriously and become a more mature professional.

I was ambitious, driven, and passionate, but I lacked discipline. And that, my friends, was key. During my entire life, discipline was the one thing that was fleeting when it came to doing things that weren't "cool," and weren't priorities to me. When I was younger I was in love with baseball. I lived for baseball - practice, playing, running, winning, losing; it didn't matter, if it had to do with baseball I wanted to do it.

But the other thing that I enjoyed more than baseball was leading the pack. To my detriment, or not, I never was a follower. And believe me, I feel that we all are followers in some way, at some point. But, in my mind, I wasn't. I believed in setting the temperature in the room at an early age. No matter the endeavor, I was going to speak up first (more than likely) and guide us in the direction I envisioned.

So as a newly hired management analyst, I had a lot to learn - especially about discipline. Having the discipline to do something that required focus and follow-through was not my strong point if it was not something that I believed was "important". Now, I know that was a horrible way to think about things, but that's what it was. I moved fast, wanted more, but had to do it my way or it was the highway.

Shortly after the encounter with my supervisor about reconciling positions, I reconnected with a childhood friend back in Atlanta. He was recently appointed to head up the budget and policy department for the City of Atlanta government and he was putting a team together to lead the agency into the future. I was excited for him and I shared how my current team was involved in cutting edge initiatives in policy and performance management as well. He was interested in this for his new team and asked would I be interested in coming down to meet his team and see what they were doing.

A trip back to Atlanta sounded great to me. I could see my family and friends, and see some new things that they were doing in Atlanta government. It was a win-win in my book. Little did I know that his invite was an opportunity for us to begin a process that would result in a major moment in my life. But hey, what great story doesn't have a surprise or two built in the plot.

Meanwhile, as we planned for me to travel to Atlanta to visit with his team, I was up to my own ambitious endeavors. Our team in Charlotte was going through a realignment and I was very interested in becoming a senior management analyst. Even though I had been there less than a year, I believed that being a senior analyst would give me some clout and I wanted to move up. My supervisors felt otherwise; and fast forward fifteen years, I agree, LOL.

I sat in the office of my then boss and asked him about placing me in the role of senior management analyst. I even had a plan to negotiate for the title in lieu of monetary gains. I was willing to just be named senior management analyst without the monetary increase. At the time I was adamant. I was in a place of instant gratification and I was determined that if I wasn't going to be promoted then someone out there in the world would want me.

What I hadn't contemplated was that I needed to learn more - to understand more. But at the time, as in life, I wasn't in a place to hear the rational voices. I was going to leap and find out just what *learning* meant to an overtly ambitious, undisciplined go-getter.

Right about the time that I was told that I would be staying in my same role, the city of Atlanta came calling because that friendly trip turned out to be a final interview for my new position - more money and the most tremendous responsibility of a lifetime at the young age of twenty-eight. I was so excited. I remember when and where I found out. I was in Durham, NC for the CIAA festivities and I received a call from my soon to be boss. He let me know, "If you want to be here with us, we want you to come." I said "yes." And it was a moment that would soon be one of the transformative decisions of my life.

This opportunity taught me a tremendous lesson. When we are resilient and we push through the obstacles, life will undoubtedly present us with the pay-off that can be even more rewarding than we initially envisioned. When I began the journey of acquiring an internship with the county manager's office in Charlotte, I didn't see that role turning into a city leadership job in Atlanta. Up until that point, all I knew was that I wanted that internship more than anything. Imagine if I would have given up after the first time I was turned down for that job. I went from job rejection to an internship, to having a senior leadership role in one of the most well-known cities in the world. Resilience is more than just fighting through the tough stuff; it's having the courage to put yourself in uncomfortable positions to achieve extraordinary goals. You have to believe that every endeavor is an *I'm-possible Opportunity.*

My time in Charlotte was coming to an end. And though I hadn't received the promotion that I wanted, it didn't matter at that point that I didn't get it. There was no need to wrestle with the whys; the fact was, I was about to leave Charlotte and set out on a journey that I would find out just who I was on the inside.

Everyone told me that I should stay (my colleagues that is). The county manager told me that it would be a mistake to leave; that true learning takes place when we stay the course. And I could tell he was not happy with me. This is the person that welcomed me in when people kept saying no. He gave me an opportunity to learn more and here I was jumping ship. But in my gut, right, wrong, or indifferent, I knew that I had to leave if I was to grow in the way that I needed to grow.

My supervisor quietly supported me, but I knew he had his reservations. I understood that he wouldn't disparage me or discourage me, but I felt he didn't agree with my decision. Again, I understood but the more the days passed, the more my mind and heart were clear. I had to go. It was time to do the necessary living and required learning that I needed to mature, become a better person, and a more disciplined professional.

Years later, I would see the county manager at various events and conferences. And though I knew he was one to never forget, I still engaged him because I knew deep inside he always cared. No matter what, he would chop it up with me, laugh and crack jokes about life and business. I looked up to him, and he had allowed me an opportunity to succeed. I never forgot that and never will.

Later in life, he would become ill and fight a courageous fight to live and give others a sense of life. I recall running into him at a conference that he had introduced me to some thirteen years prior. By this point, his illness had forced him to occasionally use a cane. But he still looked good and still walked like a man with a purpose. I said to him, "I didn't expect to see you here." He replied with that dapper swag of his, "I just left chemo, got myself together, and headed out. I'm still going." All I could think was, that's how you live. That's how I want to live. Even in his toughest battle in life, he was still teaching me, teaching us. He took on the battle to share his love of God and his fight to live fully out on the road; he spoke everywhere he could to share his message of hope, inspiration, faith, and fight.

When I first met him I admired him for his professional accomplishments; how he had come up and made his way to the big leagues in a town that had particular rules about black men in power. But during his final months, I looked at him in a different light. I had set aside the professional admiration I once held for him. Now, I admired how he stood tall as a human being in the face of what many would call a death sentence. He owned the moment. He lifted others in his time of pain. He channeled a renewed spirit. The man that gave me an opportunity to learn when I was searching for more, completed his circle of life - giving me even more than I could have ever imagined. There aren't enough words. I know he heard me say it before, but I have to say it once more - Thank You.

As I soon realized in Atlanta, being the "boss" doesn't mean anything unless you understand what the "boss" really does. At the time, in 2005, I thought I had an idea. But in reality, I didn't have a clue. I was learning on the fly. The job was huge and I was in a whirlwind. From meeting with elected officials to implementing a new financial system to responding to the catastrophic elements of Hurricane Katrina, I was in a world of high-level government bureaucracy.

Within my first few months, I had already been charged to help support the local response to Hurricane Katrina. As the budget & policy public safety division manager for the City of Atlanta, my job was to attend to any issue and/or concern related to public safety. And Hurricane Katrina was indeed a public safety issue. Thousands of New Orleans residents had to find refuge in so many cities, including Atlanta. My supervisor came to me and asked if I would serve on the mayor's disaster response team and I was honored, to say the least.

I hadn't been in my role for more than five months and here I was about to help support getting displaced families the help they so urgently needed. But what I didn't know was that this journey would mean so much more to me personally than I could have ever known. The federal government had gone into a rapid response mode after the initial devastation. Immediately after our city team learned of the funds being made available for displaced residents who found themselves in Atlanta, our mayor and all city departments went into action.

Here I was, about to lead the city's finance department's involvement in a multi-jurisdictional, nationally funded emergency response initiative to the tune of millions of dollars. I was 29 years old and all I knew was that people were depending on me and a host of other folks to get them the monies they needed so they could survive this horrific tragedy. This was a moment to step up and be part of something greater than myself. And I was all for it. FEMA (Federal Emergency Management Agency) and GEMA (Georgia Emergency Management Agency) both were working this response. And part of my job was to partner with both agencies and their local representation to make sure that the city of Atlanta was clear on all the rules and regulations associated with spending federal emergency funds during this response.

Meanwhile, I was ingratiating myself with my corporate team and department team leaders and commissioners and chiefs. My team supervised a capital and general fund budget upwards of three-quarters of a billion dollars. We were involved with everything from public safety legislation, to pension fund liability, to multi-million dollar vendor contract negotiations. During this time I was living with my mom while I searched for a place to live. And I was living the life of a single working man. I was out every night and when I wasn't out, I was in my room with a drink in my hand. My mom walked into the room one day and asked me, "Is it necessary that you have a bottle of Scotch under the bed? It can't be in the kitchen with the other food and drink?" I was embarrassed.

Although I was having a great time, doing great work, I was still not in a place where I truly understood just how much baggage I was carrying from decades of escapism. But such was life. I used alcohol and partying to numb every single real feeling in my body that I could. But every day before I went to work I was all in; well, as much as I could be - considering. The federal government had charged us with issuing millions of dollars to nonprofits and organizations that could help provide the allowable services to displaced residents. It seemed like a fairly simple task. The government had money to give, and we just needed to get it to the people that needed it. But it was not as easy as we thought. The restrictions on the federal funds were complex and bogged down in bureaucratic nonsense.

We went to work and did all that we could. I was logging fourteen-hour days and burning it at both ends. Interestingly enough, as much as we tried, we could not get all the funds to those who needed it; we left so much money on the table and had to send back millions to the federal government. That was so defeating to me. Here I was, managing this major effort for people who needed it, and I felt that I had failed to support them. There were many players involved, but for some reason, I felt the heavy burden of failure. I don't know if it was because we couldn't get more funds to those who needed them, or was it something bigger. Deep down inside it was because I was overloaded with stuff that had me "busy" but not present. And I felt guilty. Should I have done more? Could I have done more? Who knows?

But I know that as broken and lost as those displaced residents probably felt, I was feeling the same way in an entirely different set of circumstances. I remember thinking after we wrapped up the response initiative, I needed to process what was going on with me. How could someone have so much positivity happening in their professional lives, yet be internally and personally dying inside? By this time I was in year two of my new job and had moved into my new house. For a short period of time, I thought I was happy.

After going to work, hanging out, drinking to no end, coming home, passing out, and getting up hours later to start all over again, I was done. Burned out at 30 years of age. I was just done with all of it. The repetitive cycle of being miserably unhappy. There just wasn't enough alcohol or girls or sex. I couldn't get enough challenging initiatives at work to win; I just couldn't get the high I needed to escape the inner pain I was having. To think, this was the job, the opportunity that I thought I needed because I was deserving, right? It turned out to be the job I needed to reveal more of what was happening inside of me more than anything else. The saying goes, *a crisis doesn't make you, it reveals you.*

My breaking point came when I had been sick and didn't know why. I had been under the weather and had not had a physical in so long, I just decided to go to the doctor. I told them to run all the tests they could run; I needed to make sure that my mental health had not placed my physical health in jeopardy. Because honestly, I felt like I was withering away.

They tested me for everything under the sun. I had recently started dating someone and before we started to get serious I needed to know that I was well. I remember waiting for that call from the doctor. Was I ok? Did I do too much trying to escape what was bothering me? How would my life pan out? I was in a nervous rage. And why the hell hadn't they called me yet? It had been a few days and no call. But on day four,   I stood in my office lobby speaking to the administrative assistant and my cell phone rang.   It was my doctor.   As I stood there listening to him, he gave me a rundown on all my test results, I heard him breeze through my results. Negative and all well.   And my heart sank because at that moment I knew that I needed to make some life changes and begin looking in the mirror.   I wasn't physically sick, yet, but my heart and mind were not well; and I knew that if I didn't address the root of what was hurting me, I wouldn't make it.

I resilience

Expression #2: Resilience is within each of us. Every human being has the capacity to be resilient and overcome tremendous challenges. Resilience is best described as one's ability to rebound, and/or quickly recover from an incident or difficult situation. The fact is, we are taught to set aside real hurt and emotions, while simultaneously being asked to be resilient. This reality is compounded by the fact that we seldom address the root cause of our hurt and pain in a healthy way.

Resilience, or being resilient, is not a trait that one either has or doesn't have. There is an inherent resilience in all human beings that allows us to bounce back when we get down and out. But, what happens when we can't bounce back; when the challenges seem so overwhelmingly insurmountable that we can't see clear to overcome them.

This is a moment that we all have faced at some moment in our lives. It's a moment that tests our inner-most vulnerabilities and fears. We are pushed to make courageous choices. Will we sit up, face our fear in the eyes, or will we turn away and allow ourselves to sulk in our pain and self-pity?

It doesn't matter what the challenge is, a failing career, a marriage on the ropes, or even a life-altering health diagnosis. If it's your reality, it's your pain, and it matters. How do we get through the times that press us to tap into a place in our souls that feel completely empty?

Answer the following question for yourself: How will you be resilient, <u>when you need you the most</u>?

Resilience Exercise

We all have experienced a moment when we said, "I quit...I give up...I can't do this anymore." Whether it was a job, a relationship, school, or a personal goal, we have all uttered those words. Does that make us quitters? No, but it does stay with us, and quitting starts to become easier. And the more "quitting moments" we have, we carry them with us in every relationship, in every experience we have; and until we face them head-on, we never fully recover.

Instructions: In this activity, you will identify a time in your life when you gave up on something or someone, for any reason. But, because you did not follow through, you felt a certain emptiness about it and never fully processed what happened. The fact is that you may have had what you would call good reasons to stop. Nevertheless, this activity is about reflecting, examining, and processing the underlying reasons for "why" you gave in. Be honest with yourself, but remember to also give yourself grace. We all have been here. Answer the following questions (remember, don't judge yourself here):

Q1: Who or what did you give up on?

Q2: What was happening during this period in your life?

Q3: How did you feel about the conclusion?

Q4: *What do you believe was the reason you gave up and did not push through?*

Q5: *How do you feel you can recover and move forward in your life?*

After answering these questions, what's next for you? How do you want to use the information that you answered for yourself to take the next step in your resilience? What new behaviors and habits will you integrate into your life to achieve different outcomes as new challenges arise in your life? Take the time to process your answers, your reflections, and then put one foot in front of the other and proceed to move and grow.

NOTES:

_____

_____

_____

_____

_____

_____

_____

3

PURPOSE

I Looking for my lane I

...the lane that is being created for us, charges us to be courageous enough to take the unknown and unfamiliar on-ramp...

Ava DuVernay said, "When you're in your own lane, there's no traffic." After finding out I was a healthy thirty-year-old I decided to try and find my way. It was 2007, and I had just started to date a girl that I knew from my college days. I was about to tell her that I was unemployed and going to figure out my lane. I didn't think that would go over too well. But it was what I needed and I was going for it. For my health and my sanity, it was a decision that I had to make.

There are times in life we find ourselves seeking something of meaning. We often define it as what we think it is, not what it truly is.   I was focused on a career in commercial real estate.   I had gotten the idea from a combination of experiences.   While working for the city of Atlanta, I was a member of a capital project team that supervised the construction of three new public safety facilities for the city. The project was upwards of $100 million dollars and I served as the finance lead.

After working with that team for over a year, I was amazed by how much money was made in aspects of the project that I never knew about; from the site acquisition to the architectural designs, down to the cost of construction. Also, my dad had contributed to my new found interest in real estate. After having sold my first house within seven months of owning it, (the back and forth drive from the burbs to Atlanta was killing me) my dad had influenced me to rehab a residential home.

I was super intrigued by this adventure. It seemed like a great way to make a living and I could set my own schedule. But mostly, I was pretty good at the basics...building relationships, finding valuable property, and developing financial proposals. But deep down inside of me, I thought this was a great way to reconnect with my dad. He spoke about real estate like he did many other business endeavors. It made sense to me. Find an asset, buy the asset, develop the asset, leverage the asset; easy math in my estimation.

So I began to visit California more. I could see my dad, experience the warm weather, and learn the real estate game. I was all over the map. That's what happens when you are trying to find your lane and you have no clue what street you're on.   I was back and forth between rehabbing residential, finding commercial deals, learning the game, and spending money that I hoped would turn into a career.

All this time though I was listening to my dad, trying to understand the obstacles and potholes to look out for in this entrepreneurial life. For all of his life, my dad had been an entrepreneur. He had jobs with other people but for as far back as I could remember he owned a car dealership. He bought cars, sold cars, washed cars, and towed cars (yes, he had a tow truck). If it had anything to do with a car, he either, knew about it, did it, or knew who could do it.

I admire my dad for his love of business. He always would talk about the old days when he was out in the streets hustling, making deals, and learning the game. It was cool to hear someone speak about the hustle. Initially, I wanted to mimic the hustle; eventually, I wanted to perfect the hustle.

My mom is and was risk-averse; at least from what I know about her. She always would tell me to get a good-paying job and stick with it. And she should know. She was a teacher for thirty years. Can you imagine doing one thing, for that long, and not doing anything else? I admire that as well. Both of my parents, in their own way, had their own way of living life. I often would wonder what in the hell got them together in the first place. But I learned that opposites do attract (that's an entirely different book).

I was trying so many things out for what seemed like an eternity. And the money was dwindling and fading away by the day. During this same period, the economy decided to collapse. Yep, when the economy collapses real estate goes belly up. And so went my business; my journey as a commercial real estate developer went belly up, right with the economy.

I remember sitting in a bank with a banker and my attorney after putting together what would normally be a kick-ass deal to finance; and the banker letting me know that I needed 25% down to get the deal funded. Huh!? If I had 25% I wouldn't be in here I thought to myself. And aside from the banker insulting me by asking who created the deal in the first place, now he wanted all the king's men and all the king's horsemen to fund the deal. Needless to say, we passed.

After bleeding through all my money, traveling back and forth from California, North Carolina, and Atlanta, I was spent. My journey of revealing my *why* was leaving me searching for *WTF*? So I did what every practical person does when all hell is breaking loose; I found a job.

For three months I immersed myself in a brutal job. I had taken a horrendous pay cut and I was in a position that was boring as hell. While I was twiddling my thumbs and trucking into work, I was thinking too myself how did I end up back in this hell hole. I was supposed to be out making millions and changing the world. But I was crunching numbers, sitting behind a desk, figuratively beating myself in the head.

I was miserable, depressed, sad, lonely...and any other emotional descriptor you can come up with. I was fed up but I didn't have a choice. Then, a miracle happened and the heavens opened up. I had an opportunity to get back to real estate. So I promptly left that miserable job and got to working and trying to find my way.

For about six months things were looking up but the economy wasn't adjusting like I thought it would. I was in the mix, getting properties under contract, and putting deals together. But nothing was moving. Time wasn't my friend and reality became my nemesis.

It's interesting; when you are searching for meaning in life, you can find yourself feeling like you are the loneliest person in the world. I was feeling as if I was on an island and didn't have a boat to get me to safety. But at the center of it all, I was searching for something more than just money and success. I was feeling empty even though I was doing something I enjoyed. Yet, there was no joy in my spirit. I was wandering around looking for answers in the wrong places.

The journey of life is an ever-changing and steadily evolving experience. Life, in simple terms, can feel like driving on an extremely uncomfortable rocky road. The personal search for meaning and purpose can be exhausting or exhilarating. And what I have learned over time is that if you can find the inner-strength to enjoy the bumpy ride you won't need to *find* purpose. Eventually, if you keep pushing forward, your purpose reveals itself to you.

Shortly into the second tour of duty in real estate, I received a call from a former colleague turned friend. She was having a challenge filling a position on her team and since I needed to work we started thinking about a reunion of sorts. It was the perfect situation; she knew me, I knew her, and we got along really well. All the signs were aligned and the reality was that I needed to get back to work.

The team was great. Analysts, human resource specialists, and accountants, all of whom were very experienced and very smart. I was excited to just be back in an environment that I could excel in and I had a kind of renewed spirit. The year off did me some good, even if my dad and I still weren't the best of friends. So I dove in and got to work. It was cool. We fell right back into the groove of things and started on a new journey.

My fiancée was in Durham still and I was in Atlanta working and just doing the best I could to get by. Work was good and my relationship with my supervisor was even better. She made my return very seamless and gave me the keys to the team. In return, I started to try and check in on how I was treating my team (trying to be a better leader). From previous experiences, I was known as a workaholic and pretty demanding. And during my time away I had reasoned with myself that I was missing some key attributes of a servant leader. I wanted to show I cared more. And caring more is exactly what ultimately happened.

During this same time, political rumors were circulating about one particular candidate who was preparing to make a run for the position of mayor of Atlanta. The word on the street was that he had the support of the Atlanta "old guard". We call them the old guard because they were the civil rights icons that had laid down the foundation of black leadership in Atlanta.

As I sat in the office with my supervisor, we discussed the realities of who would be the next mayor of Atlanta. Politician after politician, we went down the line and examined each one. For the life of us, we couldn't conceptualize any one of them being a representative mayor; though a couple did have better attributes than others.

So we laughed and chatted more, and debated who could be the mayor and who would be the best choice. Even though that conversation happened more than ten years ago, and lasted no more than an hour or so, I remember it like it was yesterday. And then it happened. Those moments in life that you will forever talk about, reminisce on, and tell your grandchildren about during holidays and family reunions.

My supervisor turned to me in that once in a lifetime moment and says, "Glenn, hell, you should run for mayor!" Now, if this wasn't what Steve Farber calls an Oh sh!@ moment, I don't know what is. We laughed again and then I realized there was a sense of seriousness in her voice. It was as if she was initially joking, but as the moments passed she realized that the idea was plausible. And there, at that moment, a spark was lit in me that would change the course of the following decade of my life.

At some moment in the days that followed that conversation, I began to think about the idea of running for mayor of Atlanta. Could I run? Should I run? Why would I run? After sitting with these questions, I remembered what led up to this point from the start. It was the impassioned discussion that we were having in the office that day and I must have sounded like a person who could, would, and should run for office.

The more and more I contemplated it, the more I became a believer that running for mayor was not something I could do, it was necessary for me to do. I didn't feel compelled, I felt led. In my spirit, I felt that for the previous four years I had been in a position to see the challenges and opportunities in Atlanta. That role was not preparing me to be a public administrator, it was leading me to have a voice in a political process that needed a voice of vision and passion. And that's how it felt to me.

All in all, I was convinced that there was nothing to lose by making a political run and everything to gain. I didn't have any delusions of grandeur. Friends would ask me if I thought I could win but I never once even considered losing. I was going to run for an office that I believed I could win, serve, and do a better job than anyone running. My mind was focused on running the best race anyone had ever run.

My supervisor said to me during that infamous office conversation that if I ran for office she would help me. And by God did she ever. She enlisted friends, family, and anyone who would listen to help on our campaign. For the purposes of trusted help, I enlisted my childhood friend who was in between jobs. I didn't have any money so I contracted him under the terms of paying for gas and food. We started old school, straight bare-bones, grass-roots campaigning.

Because I was an unknown in the political realm I had to gain some media attention and traction to speed up my name recognition. After connecting with some political savants, I had the opportunity to get an article written about me and the campaign. That article enabled me to get into a relatively small political forum that just happened to include the four major mayoral candidates at the time. No one knew me before that night, but after that small little forum, my name would be read alongside the likes of the top contenders for mayor of Atlanta.

Our campaign was gaining traction after the first political forum of 2009. News outlets, papers, debate committees, were all contacting me to do press and sit on debate stages with the more than sixteen people running for mayor. Soon, the number of real contenders included only five candidates and I was one of the five.

The *get out the vote* strategy for Thomas for Mayor was pretty simple. It was me and a few people calling for donations, knocking on doors and attending meet and greets. Really, in the dead of summer, I was walking down Cascade Road knocking on doors and asking people to vote for me. It was brutally hot and money was scarce, so if doors were going to be knocked on, I had to do it.

I was attending debates, civic meetings, union interviews, evening affairs, you name it I was attending it and I was working my ass off. To be fully committed to the campaign I decided to quit my job. And it didn't hurt that the city's office of the city attorney was investigating whether I could run for mayor and serve in my city role anyway. Nevertheless, I wanted to commit every minute to build up the campaign for success.

So we dialed in with a small circle of friends and family and we went to work. It was surreal, to say the least; being on television and in the major papers, and even gaining national attention for what was seen as an unlikely campaign. But we had something going; people were listening to me because I was speaking about the issues that mattered to people - that mattered to me. I was the one person on the debate stages that had served in a government administrative role, managing budgets, and policy for one of the largest divisions in the city, public safety.

I spoke from my heart because that's all I knew. I shared the facts with people on the campaign and urged them to wake up and pay close attention to what my opponents weren't saying. I challenged my opponents to speak on financial security, funding public safety and infrastructure, and leading Atlanta into the future. We battled on and off the debate stages and my inner grit was challenged and fortified like never before. I ran with no fear because I was comfortable in my skin and no one could throw me off my game. They all may have had more money but I had grit - pure, unadulterated will.

As the campaign grew, we realized that our chances of reaching the finish line were slim. Yet, we kept moving forward with the understanding that soon we would have to make a decision. The end came quick, even though we had been campaigning for almost nine months.

Broke, twenty pounds lighter and worn tired, I came to a place of realization before election day. We would be dropping out of the race and supporting a candidate. At that time I didn't know which candidate that would be but whoever it was, it would have to be a decision that I could live with and hold my head up high.

So on a clear, bright morning in June 2009 I stepped out on my front porch and answered questions about our press release announcing my candidacy withdrawal. Honestly, it was timely and a refreshing relief. We had managed to do something unheard of in Atlanta; we ruffled the feathers of the establishment. All I could do at that time was call my team and my fiancée to let them know that I had not made up my mind yet about who I would support, but I would be making a decision soon. I didn't know how many supporters I had in the city, but I did know that I could make a clear and decisive statement by supporting the person I believed could lead the city forward.

Shortly after announcing my withdrawal from the race, I knew who I would support. It wasn't a popular opinion to many. Mostly everyone thought I would support the other black male in the race who was considered to be the heir apparent. Though he would go on to win in a run-off, I decided to support the one person whom I believed would be there for the residents of the city. She was white, and a rumored conservative who lived in a majority-black city. How could she win? She was showing up in neighborhoods that didn't look like her for a long time. And to me, if you show up, that's the price of admission.

After sitting with her team, my then fiancée and I knew we had the candidate that we would support. In Atlanta, this endorsement would be considered a rebel move. Nevertheless, I truly believed that without me publicly supporting her my entire candidacy would have been in vain.

Unfortunately, the story ends in defeat. She ultimately lost in a run-off. Think about that; I know I have. In a city where an overwhelming number of its citizens are black, a white female from the north side of town came so close to becoming the first white mayor of Atlanta in over three decades. It was so close. And yet it felt so far away. Because in politics, a win is a win, and a loss is a loss.

I knew that after that political campaign that I had done the right thing. Deep down inside I also knew that God was preparing me, strengthening me up for something soon to come. When we are seeking out meaning and purpose in life, the lane that is being created for us charges us to be courageous enough to take the unknown and unfamiliar on-ramp. Focused discipline helped me to come out of that campaign fully prepared to accept the upcoming journey. Little did I know just how much I was going to need that experience of running for mayor of Atlanta as I moved forward with my life.

I purpose

Expression #3:   Purpose can be seen as the most complex, simplistic word in the human language.   It is confused with being a finite type of endeavor.   But purpose is not static, it is dynamic.   I posit that most people have more than one purpose that they find throughout their lifetime.

There isn't a day that goes by that I don't either hear about purpose or think about my own purpose in life. Everyone, no matter if you are rich or poor, young or old, black or white (you get the point), has a purpose.   No matter who you are or where you are from, the odds are that you either know or want to know what your purpose is in life.

The search for purpose seems to evolve as we move from childhood to adulthood, and that makes sense.   As children, we live our lives with a free-spirit of sorts, and rarely do you see children trying to activate their *purpose* in life (unless you are a little Tiger Woods).   As we grow up and out we begin experiencing more of life, expecting more from life, and begin to ask ourselves about our place in life.   To para-phrase Simon Sinek, *we begin asking what is my why.*

But I hear a very similar story from people...*I think I know what I want to do in life, but I'm not sure if it's my purpose.*   Well, if you want to *reveal* your purpose, you must first *reveal you.*   Yes, the first step in *revealing* yourself is reintroducing *you* to *you.*   I know it sounds kind of silly.   But after experiencing so much of life's changes, up and downs, trials, and triumphs, we tend to see ourselves from an unknown lens; where we don't recognize where we are in life, or even who we are in life. I love Simon Sinek's work on purpose. He suggests we ask about our *why*, but I am going to ask you to start with your *I*. In the next exercise, answer the following question for yourself? What is my *I*, so I can reveal my *why*?

Purpose Exercise

What it means to start with *I* is a great place to begin. In this exercise, you will reflect and examine your *I* and your *why*.

Instructions: Starting with I encompasses action and a statement of affirmation that begins with the phrase "I am". It's an activity I learned from an education diversity training. We begin by stating, "I am..." and you fill-in-the-blank. If performed authentically, you probably won't have dry eyes (or maybe I'm just emotional) but you will get what I mean if you do this exercise with all sincerity and honesty. There are no hard and fast rules here, just write down what you feel, how you feel, unfiltered, about who you are. It can reference anything you wish; pretend as if you are meeting someone for the first time and you only have a few minutes to tell them who you are.

Example: My first affirmation *"I am"* statement went like this:

"I am a son who was once searching for love...I am flawed, blessed, and curious, all at the same time. I am me. I am a lover of life, a critic, a believer in goodness. I am a friend, a learning husband, and a thankful father. I am not all that I

thought I would be but I am what I know God is shaping me to be. I am a work in progress. I am great!"

Write your "*I am*" affirmation statement here: I am...

_____

_____

_____

_____

_____

_____

_____

_____

How your purpose is revealed is a journey that every human being encounters. But many of us never take the time to think about and write down the reason(s) why we feel we are here in the world. This is an opportunity to think through why you are here...your *why* is what inspires you to get up in the morning when life may not be going so well. Your *why* is what guides your soul, reveals your gifts, and ignites your inner-most passions.

Instructions: During this exercise, you will identify and write down all the things that bring you joy and you have gratitude for. You will then cross out everything on your list that is a person, place, or thing. With what is left, you will construct a personal purpose statement.

We complete these steps to identify what brings us joy and gratefulness, aside from worldly possessions and the people in our lives. Yes, our loved ones are undoubtedly important; but what happens if we don't "have" them anymore? What happens then? Does life stop?

Here is an example of the personal purpose statement process:

Step 1 - Author's example: I am grateful for (life and God, my children, my wife, family, caring for others, inspiring leaders, servant leadership)

Step 1a - Author's example: I am grateful for life and God, ~~my~~ ~~children~~, ~~my wife~~, ~~family~~, caring for others, inspiring leaders, servant leadership. (Use the space provided below)

_____

_____

_____

_____

_____

_____

_____

_____

_____

Step 2 - Author's Purpose Statement Example: "My purpose in life is to inspire people to love more abundantly, unconditionally, and passionately, in the service and care of others."

Now, does this mean that your purpose couldn't include your family or loved ones? Of course not. But this exercise is meant to challenge you to dig deep into your spirit and reveal what truly brings you joy and gratitude from the "inside-out".

Write your purpose statement here: (think about what you wrote earlier...what brings you joy, what you are grateful for, your gifts/talents, and where you can share these with the world). Remember, your purpose can be as simple as what is sitting right in front of you...we just have to open our hearts and our minds to reveal it.

_____

_____

_____

_____

_____

_____

_____

_____

_____

After completing these exercises, you should have some meaningful revelations. If not, try it again and see what happens. These are exercises and are not meant to give you a specific direction for your life. But these exercises should provide you a framework of how to be introspective and clear-minded when it comes to defining "who" you truly are, and what you define as "purpose," aside from the people you care about and your material possessions. Write down your thoughts about what you experienced while completing these exercises. How will you utilize your reflections moving forward?

NOTES:

_____

_____

_____

_____

_____

_____

_____

_____

_____

_____

_____

4

PERSEVERANCE

I See it through I

...fear shouldn't stop us from fulfilling our purpose and using our gifts...

In a world where most things worth having aren't given to you, how you persevere through challenges reveals how much grit you have. And believe me, if you don't have grit, life will be a never-ending rocky road. Many people thought I was done, over, and burnt out because I had fought so hard and came up short in the campaign. But what they didn't know was that I am built differently. I have my moments like everyone, but quit is NOT in my vocabulary. How about you? How much grit do you have? When was the last time you had to persevere through an obstacle?

After the campaign, I was able to land a leadership role with a national nonprofit. It was an extremely exciting time, considering how the previous year had unfolded. I was ready to get back to work and move forward with my life. But the reality was, in many people's perspective, I would always be the guy who ran for mayor of Atlanta and lost. I respected the position but I never had the awe of the role like so many people have. To me, being mayor was a job and I believed that I was qualified for the job. And when you are qualified, you should always consider applying. I know I may come across naive but that's just how I looked at it. I quickly learned that many people looked at it completely differently.

I would soon be sitting with my new supervisor and discussing my role with the organization. During the conversation, she interjected that she heard that I had run for political office. She had even checked with our corporate leaders to make sure that they could hire me. I was kind of stunned, but I guess she did live in the Atlanta metro area so it shouldn't have been that much of a shock. She learned about my run for office from another one of our colleagues who did what so many people do nowadays...they Google you, LOL. Yes, that's how I was found out. Someone googled me. That was ten years ago and I wasn't aware that googling someone was a thing. Well, in 2020, it's more than a thing!

My new job was really interesting. I was a regional associate director in the agency development department of a national mentoring organization. My job was to work with chief executives and board leaders in supporting their organizational development needs. It required me to consult and build relationships, and I loved it. This was the first job since my time as a founding nonprofit executive that I felt in my lane. I was comfortably uncomfortable. The best way to describe my job...I was like a coach, mentor, and thought-partner all in one. But it wasn't just what I was able to provide that was so exciting, it was the reciprocal value that I received from these amazing leaders. They filled me with so much knowledge from their lived experiences.

The dynamics of my organization were new to me. Although I had grown up in very diverse institutional surroundings, this was my first job where I was the lone black male. Out of about twenty national agency development associates, I was the one. And though it didn't bother me, I noticed it. When we would meet at our national headquarters it was quite evident that there were only four people of color in the room. Our small group had our own little code. We knew they knew, but we all acted as if it was all good. And honestly, it wasn't all good. But we did the best we could with what we had.

A major part of our job as regional directors was travel; circuit travel to be more specific. And some times circuit travel included our entire southeast team of four traveling together. I enjoyed them. I felt like we were a mini family. And when you travel together and spend the time that we spent together, you kind of are a family.

One trip, my supervisor asked me to accompany her to Louisiana. We would travel through the state beginning in New Orleans. It sounded like fun to me. It was also a full-circle moment. It was 2010 and five years post Hurricane Katrina. I would have the first opportunity to see how the city was rebounding after my involvement in Atlanta's support response initiative. In New Orleans, we were scheduled to meet with the then CEO of the local affiliate. They had experienced an extraordinary amount of organizational devastation. Financially and programmatically they were still recovering five years later and I was emotionally connected to the city; so I looked forward to seeing how they were doing, and hoping that we could support them in their efforts to stabilize the organization.

After arriving in New Orleans, we were there in the office of the CEO. It was a make-shift temporary office, the hurricane had displaced them physically as well. We entered the small office and sat down with the CEO to talk. As we sat there the conversation took its normal course. My boss started with some standard questions. And it seemed as though the CEO was doing fine. But the temperature in the room began to feel hot, and I don't mean the actual heat in the room. Again, I wasn't new to the reality of being the only Black person in a room of White people; but I didn't think that was happening in that moment.

About fifteen minutes into the meeting, the CEO of the agency abruptly says, "The way he is looking at me...he is making me nervous." I thought to myself, why would he be doing that - making her nervous that is; but then I quickly realized that she was talking about me. Hold up! Me? Ok, now I was really confused. What had happened between the time we had exchanged pleasantries and now? I hadn't said much at all in the meeting. My supervisor was doing all the talking for the most part. What was going through her mind that she believed it was ok to allow those words to come out of her mouth?

Did she think I was looking at her in a certain way? What had happened? I was lost and in disbelief. I think what was even more telling was that my supervisor looked equally stunned. From the time she uttered those words time stood still. It seemed as though an hour of pure silence had gone by...but it was only thirty seconds. And by this point, someone had to say something. So since I was the obvious "culprit" of this uneasy, uncomfortable situation, I asked my supervisor if she felt as though I should step out of the room.

I'm not sure if she said yes before she got up to get the door for me. It was seriously the most uncomfortable moment I have ever had in my professional life. I was stunned, my boss was stunned, and all I could do at the moment was shake my head in disbelief.

But once I gathered myself in the next room, I immediately went into action and phoned a friend. "What the hell just happened?" I quietly yelled into the phone. I thought, what year is it? What decade is it? I was sitting there, listening to her speak and I made her uncomfortable...ok, here we go. I thought that I had seemingly escaped the overt acts of racism and stereotyping of black men.

But maybe it was something else. Maybe she didn't want to admit in front of me that they were running the organization into the ground. That could be it, right? Whatever it was, my emotions had gone from empathy to rage in a split second. Honestly, it didn't matter at that point. I was out of the room and what was done was done. It didn't matter the excuse that would soon be thrust upon me - in my mind, I was the guy that was just reminded that he was indeed Black in America. And that was all I needed to realize that I hadn't been *present* in a nation that still battled stereotypes and racism; this was the disruption that was long over-due for me. I was a Black man in a culture that still struggled to see me as human...I was "threatening" - period. And my background meant nothing In that moment. And so I had my awakening; and I knew that my future would test me to see my way through the bigotry and ignorance that still plague America.

Earlier in that week my supervisor and I had been traveling throughout Louisiana visiting various affiliate agencies. During these trips, we usually talked shop, religion, and even politics sometimes. But this day, we ended up traveling down a path of hidden treasure. We started talking about family. Yes, I know, not the smartest topic to engage in, especially considering my pinned up emotional history.

But we went *there*. She ended up asking me about my dad and I remember thinking that I could talk about him as long as I just kept it simple. As we discussed the realities of growing up with parents, not in the household, I found myself sinking into a place of despair and emotional torment.

Once again, the past became real and once more I revealed to myself that I was hurt beyond measure. I remember vividly staring out of the car window as we pulled into a new city, preparing to exit the off-ramp. My eyes were full of water such that I had to keep my head turned to my passenger window to block the view from tears rolling down my face. Thank God I wasn't driving this time; I could only imagine the spectacle that would have been.

From realizing that I was still a Black man in America, to struggling with my father-son relationship, I needed to get it together. I needed to get stronger - to heal - to wake up.

Yeah, I knew of the realities of America. But when you have intentionally blocked out ignorance and stupidity all of your life, you can become blind to what is staring you in your face. I was confronted with the realities that no matter what I did, America saw me as a threat; and no matter how hard I tried, it seemed as though my dad did not see me at all. In that moment, I didn't know which reality hurt the most.

It was deeper than I thought; deeper than what I wanted to tackle. But that's the crazy thing about our demons - the things that stay with us in our sub-conscious. They are there for as long as we allow them to be. Being woke, present or conscious has little to do with intellect; it has everything to do with personal will, determination, and courage.

Sometime later I would find out that I was going to be part of a reduction in force after 2 1/2 years on the job. Unfortunately, I found out on my birthday trip. Fortunately, my birthday trip happened to be in the Bahamas. So, such is life, I ventured out on a new path. I gave myself the strong man talk and decided to man up and get to work. It was time for me to move from being comfortably uncomfortable to focusing my mind on the future with more intention.

Prior to being laid off, I had continued to be involved with civic committees in Charlotte. That was something that was in my DNA. I was an appointed member of the city's community relations committee. Shortly after taking the job with the national nonprofit my wife and I had relocated to Charlotte. It was a good move for both of us. She needed out of Atlanta and I needed to resettle and refocus. I had friends in Charlotte and had briefly spent time working for the county so it just made good sense.

When I returned from the Bahamas I knew I wanted to land somewhere that would bring me a sense of purpose. Coincidentally, I had been serving on a subcommittee that was comprised of several Charlotte organizations. One of those organizations was a very influential community nonprofit. A close acquaintance was the representative for the nonprofit at that time I served as co-chair; and for the most part, my main role on the subcommittee was to play facilitator for the various agencies that collaborated for the annual MLK celebration. It can get contentious when people want what they want. So my consultant calm demeanor had to be present in the room at all times.

An acquaintance emailed me after I emailed my committee letting them know that I was transitioning from my job. He had recently listed a job opening to lead one of his teams at (what I will call the "Center"). I was interested and it seemed like a perfect fit for me. I would be working to build relationships across the organization while overseeing community programs and partnerships to increase the value that the *Center* brought to the Charlotte community. It seemed like a match made in heaven and the timing was perfect.

A couple of months after he had reached out to me I was introduced as the new director. It was pretty cool. I had grown up in a similar organization in Atlanta, attending sports programs, teenage dances, and swimming. It felt like I had come full circle once more. From the beginning he let me know that my job was to first build relationships - to build trust. "Take it slow," he would tell me. But I was a go-getter. How would this work? But of course, I agreed and I went to work, learning the people, the culture, and politics. We had a pretty big responsibility. Most of all the education-based community programs fell within our wheelhouse. And the donors enjoyed being part of this community impact. So I took the job seriously; probably too serious as I would end up realizing.

Our team was made up of two divisions, the program, team, and the support team. Interestingly enough, the program team was an all Black female team except for one white female, and the support team was all White females.

It didn't bother me that this was the make-up of the team, except that anyone with a partially clear eye could see that there were stark differences in how each team operated, and how they were treated by the organization.

Ok, here we go down this road; you may not want these truths. So here is how this went down. Remember, when leaning into discomfort, your *will* has to be strong! So as I was learning the PPC (people, politics, culture) of the *Center*, I began to realize some things. Once again, my awareness of the organizational culture was drastically misunderstood; at least in organizations that I had my biases about. This was a faith-based organization founded on principles and beliefs rooted in Christianity. But the *Center*, as in all organizations, was (is) imperfect.

Don't get me wrong, just because the organization was flawed, doesn't mean the people were all flawed. I found some amazing people there, including my boss. He supported my every move even if he disagreed. It was refreshing. But the stubborn in me would eventually get the best of me in a pretty sweet situation. You see, when your stubborn self meets your ambitious self, mixed in with a little unresolved emotional childhood trauma, you get a whole heap of mess.

So about halfway into my time in the role, our community programs were growing and more attention was being garnered from donors and the community as a whole. Our team was encouraged and the *Center* leadership was becoming more supportive. During the same time, I was aware of some disparities in some of the personnel matters within our program and support teams. It made me uncomfortable and at a minimum, I questioned the appearance of such differences in the treatment of the people involved.

The program team and support team sat in the same office area, and there was one support staff team member that seemed to be treated differently than everyone else. I liked her for what it was worth, but I would always hear that she let the team know in her own way (being too frank mostly), just how much she differed from everyone else. There were talks of the inequities in the office that were seemingly drawn across racial lines. I became more and more frustrated as I learned more details. And as a war of words and deeds played out secretly behind closed doors, I became incensed.

After working on a funding proposal for our community programs, our team was awarded a major federal grant. I was super excited. Not only would we have an opportunity to serve more kids, but it would also prove to the executive leaders that we did indeed bring value to the *Center*.

But the internal rifts continued. And because I was having tremendous challenges with his outlook on the matter (among other challenges I was having), my boss felt as though it would be a good idea for me to have a 360 degree-professional assessment done for my one year anniversary. And I'm sure some folks in the association had already been sharing their two cents on my very unique way of engagement. By this point, I was open to it. I had never had a 360 done and I needed someone to talk with about the crazy stuff happening in and outside of work. It was his decision for me to have this done for all those reasons and more.

An incident had preceded him finally deciding to have my 360 completed. After having a crazy day at work, I was feeling this entire *racial thing*; and on top of what was perceived to be special treatment for some, I had just about had enough. I walked up to his office one evening and what commenced was an unleashing of emotions, anger, and frustrations released all on my boss. He sat speechless for much of it - and the look on his face was priceless for sure.

I had just ripped my boss for making decisions that he in fact could make. I ripped into him for doing what he had the prerogative to do and didn't have to check with me one bit. I couldn't tell if he was upset or hurt. After I walked out of his office I vaguely remember that he didn't say much. My temper was on twenty so I really couldn't recall what even really happened. I jetted out of the building, proceeded to call my wife, and emotionally shared with her that I would most likely be getting fired in short order. The only question was if they would offer me a severance.

That meeting was a super defining moment for me in my life. Even as they provided me an executive coach (because I needed one), I still wasn't putting one and one together. I was adamant that he had not made the best choices when it came to our team even though he was supportive of me as their leader.

At my exit lunch (because you know that's where this ended up), I shared with him my disappointment and frustration about how I felt that preferential treatment was being given to some (White women) and others (Black women) were being excluded. I went on and on about how I couldn't be a part of an organization that didn't do right by its team - all of the team.

But the underlying reason as to why I was so mad, so angry and frustrated the entire year, wasn't solely because someone was being treated differently. I had seen that happen before; it wasn't because one group was white and the other black. These issues were important for sure but they didn't warrant my rage. They warranted truth and reason, and a leader that could articulate what was fundamentally wrong with the circumstances and a solution on how to fix them.

However, remember, hurt people - hurt people. And I was still very hurt "below the iceberg," where no one could see but I could feel. I was mad at him, not because of all the team dysfunction, but because he hadn't responded the way I wanted him to; because when I pointed out something I deemed important, he didn't move quickly enough. I wanted him to respond the way my dad never responded. I wanted affirmation. I needed him to see what I saw and acknowledge it. And because my boss chose to be his own person, to be my supervisor and make decisions he believed were appropriate, I acted out as any five-year-old child would.

It was like that old saying, *it's me, not you.* I believed the team dysfunction was real, and I was angry because unbeknownst to him he reminded me of a father who wouldn't love me through affirmation and acts. Two things can be right at the same time. My supervisor was a man in a position of power, that I disagreed with; and he didn't stand a chance. I was hurt, angry, and broken, and couldn't decipher how to be a leader in a moment that required me to be an adult in the room. I wasn't honest with myself in those moments; my will had faltered and my awareness was completely absent. But no matter what happened, I would have to find a way to get through this. I was being blessed with these amazing opportunities, yet I was struggling because I had not addressed all the stuff that was below my surface.

Perseverance isn't solely about getting through professional storms; it's just as, if not more, important to persevere through the personal ones as well. And this was one of those experiences that revealed to me that I needed to get present and truthful about what was holding me back. I had to get honest and self-aware about my hurt and pain that was being misdirected. Look, if you have ever had an "aha" moment that shook your world up, then you know what I'm talking about. When these moments happen, we have to summon the courage to deal with our personal stuff so that we can step into the blessings that are waiting for us.

I perseverance

Expression #4: If you have ever quit at something that you feel that you should have stayed the course, that was a moment that you probably felt like you lacked perseverance. Perseverance is a quality that is easier to discuss, and hard as hell to exhibit. Perseverance is best described as one's ability to simply see anything through to completion.

In college, I pledged the Omega Psi Phi Fraternity at NC Central University. For several reasons, that will mostly be left unsaid, my line name ended up being *Perseverance*. I had been trying for two years to become an Omega man and I refused to give up no matter the roadblocks. I wanted to become an Omega since I was in middle school. So you see, there was nothing that was going to stop me. After a while, my then big brothers could see that quit was not in my vocabulary.

In life, we sometimes face extreme situations that require us to summon a tremendous amount of courage. Sometimes we will fall short. But what is it about those times that render us unable to push through to the end? How is it that we sometimes find the inner warrior and other times we don't? Is it that we aren't built the way we think we are? Or is it more complex?

If it is more complex then don't we owe it to ourselves to understand what it takes to strengthen and activate the muscles that will empower us to achieve our most ambitious goals? I say yes we do. We can all persevere. Maybe we don't win every single time, but we can for sure persevere and increase our odds for success.

Fear is real and in some cases necessary. Fear should help us from making irrational decisions, like walking into a street of moving cars. But fear shouldn't stop us from fulfilling our purpose and using our gifts. The idea that we shouldn't ever have fear is nonsense. Yet the proposition that *using fear* to inspire and motivate us to reach our audacious goals is the direction I want us to reach for. *Answer the following question for yourself: How will you persevere in life to achieve what God has in store for you on the other side of fear?*

Perseverance Exercise

When the time comes for you to fight through self-doubt, what will your perseverance muscles be prepared to endure? This exercise will help you develop, strengthen, and activate your perseverance muscles when you need them the most.

You may be familiar with the acronym SMART when speaking of goals. SMART stands for specific, measurable, attainable, relevant, and time-based. These are all very important factors in setting goals. But, because this book is entitled, "*Heart Work*," I want to offer you an exercise that challenges you to set some HARD goals: heartfelt, animated, required, and difficult (Murphy, 2010). In Mark Murphy's (2010) *Hard Goals: The secret from getting from where you are to where you want to be,* he outlines a very simple yet meaningful equation to achieving your most audacious goals. I personally love this strategy because I am all in for setting goals that are driven by the heart.

Instructions: Answer the questions (Murphy's HARD outline below) for each step in setting your HARD goal(s). For the next 90 days work on achieving this goal. This goal should be something that you genuinely want to accomplish but for whatever reason, real or otherwise, you have yet to begin. It should be a goal that can be accomplished within 90 days, because 90 days is realistic, and if you falter (which may happen), you can quickly get back on track.

In his *Forbes* article *HARD Goals, Not SMART Goals, Are the key to career development*, Murphy (2017) outlines how he recommends we specifically go about setting our HARD goals *(the following questions have been adapted for the purposes of this exercise)*:

Q1: Animate - Imagine where you want to be in your life (personally, professionally, etc.) and design in your mind what it looks like. Be specific, use affirmative words, and be clear on what you want to see happen. What is your 90-day goal?

Q2: Heartfelt - Describe why this goal is important and meaningful to you. What is it about this goal that pulls at your emotions and keeps your attention? Why does this goal connect with your heart?

Q3: Difficult - What skills will you need to develop/ leverage to overcome the challenges/obstacles that you will undoubtedly face?

Q4: *Required - What do you need to accomplish in the next 24 hours to begin your journey to unleashing your greatness, achieving your audacious goal? What is required of you in the next 30/60/90 days?*

As you experience this exercise, try not to be concerned about what you think your goal(s) should be, but rather what your heart wants them to be. Take this opportunity to lead with love, be inspired by your heart, and allow your passion to be present at the moment that you are envisioning your future.

NOTES:

_____

_____

_____

_____

_____

_____

_____

5

LOVE

I Love matters I

...love is hard because it challenges us to be unconditionally selfless when we secretly want to be selfish...

. . . .

Shortly after I parted ways from the *Center*, I started my new job at major retailer, *Big Red* (yes, it's another made-up name to protect the innocent). I had been encouraged to apply for a leadership role there by a friend of mine; all this was happening while I was at the *Center* and so it was fitting that once *Big Red* offered me a job I would find my way to remove myself from the crazy show that was happening in my life.

Who would have thought that a chance encounter in the grocery section of a store would lead me to become a general manager for a major retailer? Not me and definitely not any of my former colleagues. Before leaving the *Center*, my wife and I had given birth (and by that I mean she gave birth) to a baby boy named Grayson (named after my grandfather) and we were adjusting to all the newness in our lives.

My training schedule had me working abnormal business hours for the most part, and I soon would come to realize that the slogan "retail is hell" was very accurate. But what I began to understand was that retail was less about selling stuff and all about serving people. My training partner was a veteran general manager and he had it perfected. He was direct, semi-serious funny, and moved really fast. In retail you have to move fast, everything is always moving, going, and shifting. And he moved right along with it. When we first met I could tell he was thinking, 'this dude won't last'. But I wasn't concerned. I knew that there wasn't a job created that I couldn't excel at. And honestly, at that time, for what they were paying me I would have just about done anything to succeed (or so I thought).

As I was learning the ropes at work, walking around a super retail store for ten hours a day, I was attempting to learn how to be a dad. It was tough. I never really imagined getting married, let alone having a child. I think I was in shock so much that I welcomed the newness of the job because it kept me busy and I didn't have time to think about the life that I was responsible for; I just had to go to work and raise my kid the best I knew how.

Grayson was not the best sleeper and so began the road to sleepless nights and weary days. But he had the biggest smile and he was all pure love, rolled up into a bundle of seven pounds. How could so much joy exist in something so small? It was so beautiful to be holding him and playing with him, and all the while I would ask myself, "Is this what my dad did with me?"

The voices in my head began to speak to me heavily, so much so that I started to try and fill the voices with distractions (again). Back and forth to work and home, I was busy and my wife was exhausted. But I had to push through - we had to push through because there were three of us now, not two.

At work I was finding out how to do all sorts of things, the most interesting of all was learning the back room. I mean, you talk about being scared to kill somebody; you needed to be certified to maneuver through there...no, seriously, you had to get certified to use those machines. And I was sure that I would be fired for my inability to learn how to move those boxes onto those high shelves.

From folding shirts to stocking shelves, cashing guests out, and even sweeping floors, I was learning it all. And the crazy thing was, I was enjoying it. It wasn't that it was 'menial labor,' it was that I was doing work that was necessary for everything in the store to work well. I had a sense of pride in knowing that all the little things added up to an amazing experience for those who came in to shop the store. I recall a friend asking me why I wanted to work in retail as if it were a low-level job. But the real treat was that I was able to work alongside people that I rarely had an opportunity to work with.

The real champions of our world; working-class champions. These champions were folks that didn't get paid high salaries and in most cases didn't make a fair hourly wage. But they worked their butts off because they had lives, families, bills, and they mattered.

When I took the job I remember the recruiter telling me that retail was more than selling stuff; that my desire to inspire people, lead people, and learn from people would be my greatest experience. Quickly, I found that he was right on the mark. I was in a place, a position, that was surely going to change me forever for the good.

During my three month training period, I had time to get to know my trainer. Imagine shadowing someone for three months, more than fifty hours a week for five days a week. We had some deep conversations and during my training period I felt *me* growing inside in a way I never knew could or would happen. Coming out of the previous situation I hadn't yet wrestled with my accountability in that debacle, and my trainer was a new voice and sounding board with no judgment and no axe to grind.

So I did something that was rare for me, I began a journey of being vulnerable and honest with someone other than God. Typically, one would think that it wouldn't be the best idea to divulge deep dark secrets about yourself, but at some point in life, your past is either helping you or hurting you. Mine was doing the latter. So I decided to just be me, starting with some truths.

My trainer had kids, was married, and found it in himself to share some of his life with me. Over time we began to trust one another. It was strange at first, that this older white dude who had spent most of his life in retail had forged this relationship with a younger black dude who had only shopped retail for most of his life. But friendships blossom out of the strangest circumstances sometimes. And this friendship was genuinely built on a connection of trust.

After a couple of months, I began to work shifts as manager by myself; he would have an opportunity to take vacation, and do some other things that he wanted to take time to complete. The time for me to showcase my skills had quickly stumbled upon me. I was leading a retail store by myself without the cover of my trainer...and yes, I was nervous. But he had been an amazing trainer so I was ready for the challenge.

My first day leading the team by myself was humbling, to say the least. I had come so far in a role that was challenging me on so many levels. The team members, however, by this time had begun to trust me. They saw how hard I worked and they still pushed me. I had to earn my wings in that environment and I was up for the challenge. I would walk the store, inspect products on the shelves, and assist guests. But really, the most important thing that I did in that building was to connect with my team. That was my most important job every day, every time that I stepped foot into that store. Who would have ever guessed? I was paid quite well to wake up in the morning, go to work, and demonstrate to the best of my ability that I cared for my team. I was beginning to understand what leadership was really about.

And at home, the arrival of my new baby boy was still becoming real to me, and it was changing me too. I was experiencing a life shift in two areas of my life; becoming a father and becoming a servant leader. God was stepping in, on his time-line, at the right time and I was in for an amazing journey.

My training had consisted of spending time with each department in the store, including human resources. And I learned a hell of a lot. But what I took away from the technical learning is that details are critically important; not because they are business-critical but because if we can get them right we can serve our teams better. It was the first time that I was able to correlate being detailed oriented to *serving*. That was a powerful moment for me.

So when I was leading the store myself, I began to rethink what leadership was for me - for the people I aimed to serve. Was it simply knowing the business, driving performance, and leading the team? Or was there more? I believed there was so much more. I had realized that leading wasn't about what I knew, it was about how I lifted others up. I stopped and asked myself, "Who had I lifted up in my life?" And there was my gut-check - not many. I had helped people get jobs, mentored some folks, and even kept in contact with people who needed guidance occasionally; but I had not lifted someone by helping them to develop their skills and gifts so they could transform their lives. I had not loved my teams to reach their greatness - what they were created to be in life. This was another oh sh!@ moment for me.

So this is where I began to rethink me, my life, and my purpose on this earth. In a retail store in North Carolina...wow, the strangest stuff can happen in the most unlikely places. And here I was about to begin living life on the terms God had designed, not me. At that moment, the burden of hurt, fear, insecurities, and trauma was slowly being lifted off of my heart. The reality of what was happening was clear...I was able to receive the notion of helping to lift someone else because I was being freed from the burdens I had been carrying for so long.

After attending a regional meeting with my district leader and general manager colleagues, I was told that I would continue to work at my training store until a store became available for me in Charlotte, NC. It sounded good to me. I had a new baby and a marriage that required a checkup so I was all in for not having to relocate. But remember this, tell God your plans and He will indeed laugh out loud. Soon after our meeting, I jumped in my car to return home; but before I could reach the highway two blocks up the road, my district leader called me and asked me to pull my car over. Huh? Pull the car over? Now either I was about to be terminated or I had just hit the lottery and he didn't want me to wreck in my ecstatic joy.

But neither was true (I wished I had hit that lottery though, for real). He calmly said, "Glenn, how would you feel about moving to Greensboro?" These words would be the start of the next chapter of personal struggle, professional growth, and an extreme test in faith, family, and mental health. I paused. And after he gave me the specifics (sales pitch), I said yes. And so began the next chapter.

After convincing my wife that Greensboro was the place we would need to move, she agreed (unenthusiastically that is) and we started to get ready for a move eighty miles up the road. Getting my stuff in order was a key priority for this move and I was about to set our family on a real game of March madness.

We were scheduled to land in Greensboro in February 2014, but while planning the move I had decided to head up to Greensboro to meet the team and check out the store. It would be my way of developing relationships before my official start. On my way to Greensboro, the weather started to get bad and I started to see snow on my drive up the highway. But I figured I would go up and turn around pretty quickly; no harm, no foul.

After staying in Greensboro for a few hours, I decided (or the weather decided) that it was time for me to hit the road to get back home to be with my wife and son. Half-way into my drive, I felt conflicted. Would I leave the new team, that I had just met, with the challenge of holding down the store without me? Or would I call my wife and baby boy and ask them to hold down the fort while I went to help my new team? I know what you may be thinking...who wouldn't go home?

But I had signed up for this life, to serve people even when it meant my family would have to wait for me. I realized that I had signed my family up too and my heart was heavy. I couldn't start this new relationship off with my team by heading home when they had to leave their families at home and weather the storm.

So I called my wife, turned the car around, and went back to the store. My boss told me to not worry about coming back, but I just couldn't bear being in the comfort of my home while my new team was working their butts off. When I stepped into the store, many of the team members were shocked but I could also tell that they were happy I was there. I'm sure they could have held things down, they were a pretty seasoned group; but there's something to be said when you have the entire team in the building with you. It means something more; I get it because it means something to me.

We would fight off that storm together, serve our guests, and build the type of camaraderie that develops in the toughest situations. After leaving to head home I had mixed feelings. I had left my family to be at work and I know they needed me just as much as my job did. And I knew that wouldn't be the last time I would have to make that type of decision. My private prayer was that it would be easier in some way, but that was me being hopeful and mostly naive.

I never thought about the relationship between love and leadership in the beginning of my career. But now, having this role at *Big Red* was leading me to understand that love was essential in leading. I began to think more about how I was showing up for my team and how I wanted to show up in the future. But this was love at its core; sacrificing for others because it's what they need and want, not what you want.

Once our family was settled into Greensboro, the work of leading my new family was beginning. And from the start, I knew I was going to need a major dose of patience and grit to make this journey a successful one. My supervisor was cool and was a fairly no-nonsense, open, a matter of fact kind of guy. He was former military and had been with the company for a few years, so he had a pretty good grasp on the work. He was supportive from the start, giving me the space and time to feel and figure some things out on my own.

Less than thirty days in my new role, my wife walked into the bedroom at about 1 am and looked at me with tears of panic in her eyes, "I'm pregnant," she said. WTF! Yeah, it was a moment. Though I kind of suspected it, it never is real until those words come to life. Weeks earlier she had been complaining about feeling sick, similar to the first time we learned of being pregnant. So I had leisurely purchased some pregnancy tests just in case she wanted to rule out being pregnant. Those tests stayed on our counter for over a week. I think she really couldn't come to terms with the possibility of having another child while not having fully recovered from having our first child.

But as we say in my frat, running from it will not save you. She was pregnant and it was real. Ok, let's take a moment here to digress: If you are a man who has been in this position or know of someone that has been in this position, there are some unwritten rules to how you proceed with this reality coming to light. No matter what you do, how much you think you are helping - you, as a man, cannot control how your significant other is going to respond in this situation. The best thing you can do is say thank you...then open your ears, open your heart, do your best, and be as patient for as long as you can; and then be patient some more. Me - I failed this test horribly, but I tried nonetheless.

Now back to the originally scheduled story. In a retail culture, as in most business cultures, there tend to be three divisions of people: those who like you, those who don't like you, and those who hate you. I know what you're thinking, what happened to the 'those who don't care'? Everyone cares and everyone has an opinion no matter what they say. So I knew that these realities existed - the question would be, to what degree did they exist and how would I handle it.

After about three months on the job, I believed that most of my team liked me. But there were a few that were on the fence, just trying to figure me out. And then there were a couple that hated me. And I do mean hate. The problem with these two was that they were direct reports and they were my connection to the larger team. If they hated me, their influence would be detrimental to the culture of the team. But

I knew from my past experiences that people who hate you - when they don't know you, are dealing with stuff that has nothing to do with you.

I would sit in my office with one of these leaders who disliked me to the end of the earth; she would cry when we would discuss her work performance. Initially, I thought that she was just not used to having someone critique her work and she was responding emotionally because this was new to her. But over time I started to see that she just wasn't emotionally mature. She lacked emotional intelligence; and in her eyes, I was the bad man telling her she wasn't good enough. I tried everything; taking things off her plate, reassuring her that she was doing well, and even taking her to lunch to try and build a relationship.

Once, at lunch, I flat out asked her, "Do you even like me?" And she bravely responded, "Nope." Yes! Thank God for an honest response I thought to myself. But I knew that her not liking me had nothing to do with me. How did I know that? Well, remember, I had my moments too; back at the *Center* in Charlotte when I railed on my boss - that had nothing to do with him. So what did I do at that moment? Nothing, I thanked her for being honest and assured her that I would do all that I could to support her, and let her know that I would help her find her professional way because I knew that she didn't want to be there anymore.

Soon she would resign and move on to something different professionally. I wasn't hurt or upset. I knew that something was happening with her - had happened to her, that had nothing to do with me. All I could do was be empathetic and aware that I wouldn't compound her inner stress with additional stress.

Yes, my new way of leading was called *leading with love*. You may ask how I came up with this new way of leading. Remember, I had found something new during my training; things began to make sense for me. I knew that leading a team of people who could easily go work somewhere else and make the same or more money would require something different; and I had to understand that the only thing that would matter was to be present with them - to genuinely care for them; to passionately lead with love. It wasn't for everyone...but it was certainly for me.

It was 3 AM and I sat in my car waiting for the morning leader to arrive for the early team. During this time of day, only the team members who unloaded the truck came to work and I was there to assist them. At first, my team thought I was coming to check in on them since I didn't have to arrive until 7:30 AM. But I was there because I had made a commitment to my team and myself: I would be present on every shift at some point, learn the business, connect with teammates, and demonstrate my commitment.

The idea that a general manager would come to work so early, and not only be there with the team, but actually be on the truck - moving and throwing boxes, and actually working was simply unheard of. But I wasn't there for pats on the back, I was there to do my part; to do what was required of all leaders who seek to lead with love.

The experience of sacrificing time, sleep, comfort - aka privilege, was all worth it for the opportunity to be present with my team. Meanwhile, back on the home front, my wife, son, and 'baby to be' were living another life. I was at work for ten to twelve hours a day, and though I wasn't absent from home I vaguely remember being present. It was if I was winning at work and losing at home. And that dynamic is a losing proposition.

Right before we arrived in Greensboro, our company had experienced a financial breach and it had affected guests everywhere. It was a public relations nightmare and the complete nature of the fall-out would be unknown for months. We had to immediately find ways to restore our image, make our customers whole again if they were affected, and figure out how to bounce back financially; but more so to reclaim our brand identity.

After some months had passed, my executive team looked a little different, and I began to feel as though we were coming together as a whole unit. I had lost some team leaders, either due to performance or just not the right fit for retail. Either way, we were humming along and I was ready to introduce my philosophy of how we would stay the course and come out a top store in the company.

Most of my leadership team were hesitant at first. I mean, I did open up a team meeting talking about how we would *lead with love* moving forward. They had never in their lives heard that in a retail store or probably anywhere for that matter. But I was convinced that love was going to help us achieve the minimum performance goals of our company - but I wanted more. I wanted to exceed those goals; I wanted to kick butt and take names because I believed that we could do better than just the minimum.

My counter-parts shrugged and in some cases laughed. And why wouldn't they? I knew that policies, operation manuals, and business strategies mattered - but if these components of the business are not delivered with love they are meaningless and no ambitious goal was ever reached by being meaningless. *Lead with love* is more than just a saying, it has meaning. I asked my team to Listen, Engage, Adapt, and Deliver (LEAD) with love. If we could collectively exhibit these acts while implementing our key business strategies, and do them with love, we could achieve anything.

Over the following months, times were challenging, teams were faced with just doing the work or doing the work the right way. Over time though teammates began seeing the commitment of each leader and team member, and saw that doing the work right was the culture. So they either would join us or they would eventually find another place to work. Most of our team joined us and we forged a path to being great. Whether team leaders worked extra shifts, supported struggling teammates, called and checked on the sick, or even attended the funeral of one of our beloved teammates; whatever it took, we did it.

We were winning at work, and I was still losing at home. The birth of a newborn baby girl, Zoe, blessed us during the holiday season, and my team was concerned. *Would I be able to be there with them?* The holidays, specifically the Christmas holiday, was a major time of the year in retail and planning for the season was a priority. But my district leader saw my work ethic in action, he saw the late hours, the extra shifts, the commitment of me and my team to be the best. He told me, "Take the time to be with your family...babies are only born once."

There was indeed fallout with one of my senior leaders. She believed that I shouldn't be taking time off during the planning season for Christmas. But I was ok with that because I knew that her grief wasn't about me. Everyone else on my team was so supportive, it touched me in a special way.

One of my senior leaders was a young man who had done everything he could to be the best he could while I had been there. He shined not because he was selfish but because we empowered him to be his best self. Prior to me coming to the store, no one had been a support for him. Why wouldn't leaders support him? And again I thought to myself, *when we exact our frustrations and fears and emotional baggage on others and disguise it as "leadership," that's not about anything other than our own mess.* It's just as simple as that. That same young man is a retail store general manager today. He earned it, with commitment, perseverance, and love.

But a ton of heavy lifting later, our team had come into their own. We had finished the year strong. There we were, having taken a chance to lead with love, care for our team and guests, lift each other up, and commit to working the right way. To me, it didn't matter what the performance metrics said, I had first-hand knowledge of just what happened. Our team gave their all, to each other, to themselves, to our mission.

We ended that year as a top store in the company, achieving and exceeding every single performance metric that corporate asked us to hit. My entire team received raises and promotions and I received the biggest bonus check I had ever seen. But the greatest gift of all was seeing our team celebrate achieving the right way; by loving each other, taking care of each other, and taking care of our guests. That was it.

I was changed forever and I would never look back again. For everyone who had laughed at me, called me naive, or even just dismissed me - we did more than prove them wrong, we proved us right.

So what did I learn? I learned that love does conquer ALL. We moved mountains with love, and when in doubt I suggest you turn to love no matter how difficult the circumstances may seem. Maybe your personality doesn't fit the "love" bill, but that's not required. So what is required? Your commitment to caring and loving those you seek to serve (lead). I found that leading with love, at home, and at work, was just easier than anything I had ever done in my life. Why? Because love is just plain easy. And anger, bitterness, and resentment are simply difficult existences. We make *love* hard because it challenges us to be selfless when we desperately want to be selfish. And when we are being selfish we run the chance of being hurtful, harsh, and misguided.

Can you see yourself *leading with love*? Are you able to imagine a life where you are guided by how much and how often you love others? Trust me, it may sound pie in the sky, but I challenge you to stop making excuses on why leading can be so difficult; and start making it easier - and *lead with love*.

I love

Expression #5: Love is one of the most storied and admired words in the human language. Without it, we suffer in the human experience. That's why so many of us search for it, yearn for it, sometimes loath it even, and have a whirlwind relationship with it. Famed singer and minister Whitney Phipps says it best, *"Love is when what you want is never important, but what the other person needs and wants is always paramount."*

The Greeks defined love by four words, *storge*-empathy bond, *philia* - friend bond, *eros* - romantic love, and *agape* - unconditional "God" love (Farber, 2020). I define love as the embodiment of an experience, the caring, and connecting with another being, unconditionally. But agape love is the love that we have the greatest challenge to embrace. Why is this the case for so many of us? Why is it so difficult to love unconditionally?

For as long as I can remember I was searching for love in all the wrong places. From the age of five to my mid-thirties I was looking for love. The only problem was, I didn't know that's what I was doing. Just like a finger-print, every expression of love, for every creature that experiences it, is uniquely their own. And who, why, what, when, and how we love, can be a matter of circumstance or choice.

But have you ever encountered a time when you could have welcomed love and you chose otherwise? Maybe with a friend, in a tough situation, or with your child; when you could have easily decided to insert love but you just couldn't bring yourself to do it.

And have you ever asked yourself why you chose against love? Why not love; why the alternative? Was it just easier to be, say, or do anything but give love? It can be hard sometimes to choose the one emotion, the one act, that transcends our irrational thought. If you could choose love every day, what would your life look like? How would you feel? How would the people around you, the people you influence, and impact every single day feel? *Answer this question for yourself: What would your life resemble if you loved unconditionally?*

Love Exercise

To love unconditionally one must first be able to have the capacity to forgive. This can be a tough challenge for most if not all of us. But, if we can try to position our minds to be present, no matter the circumstances, we may be able to create in our hearts the ability to forgive what was once unforgivable.

Instructions: Write down three people (including yourself if warranted) that you have not forgiven. Detail the circumstances of the reason(s) why you have not forgiven them. (Write in the space provided here)

_____

_____

_____

_____

_____

_____

_____

_____

_____

Answer the following questions about forgiveness:

Q1: *Why is it so hard to forgive them?*

Q2: *What will happen once I forgive them?*

Q3: *How will my spirit and energy shift once I forgive them?*

Q4: *Can I forgive them?*

Q5: *If I can/can't forgive, then what happens next?*

Answer the following questions about unconditional love:

Q1: *Do I have the ability to love unconditionally? If not, why?*

Q2: *Do I need something in return when I love others? If so, why and what?*

Q3: *If I don't receive love back, is that ok with me?*

Q4: *What do I need to do to love unconditionally?*

Q5: *If I can love unconditionally, how will my outlook on life evolve?*

As you complete this exercise and answer these questions, think about how forgiveness and unconditional love currently are present in your life; then imagine how they both can inspire a life that you dream of having - a life of presence, purpose, and love. If you have difficulties working through these questions, that's ok. You don't have to answer them all at once. But don't be discouraged, keep asking yourself the questions and when you are able to answer, celebrate your wins and keep moving forward.

NOTES:

_____

_____

_____

_____

_____

_____

_____

_____

_____

_____

_____

_____

_____

_____

_____

_____

_____

_____

6

GRATITUDE

I Be still, in gratitude I

*Gratitude is the starting point of experiencing
a joyous life.*

I was standing in my kitchen, jobless, and after five years of marriage, I was still struggling to find inner peace and direction in myself. I had come to realize that I was failing at marriage and in trouble of failing at fatherhood. I felt as if I was slowly becoming an image of my worst fears...and that was a reality I didn't want, but the feeling wouldn't go away. The most difficult thing I did in those moments was admitting to myself that I was severely unhappy. And I was making my wife equally unhappy. It was if we were galaxies apart and I didn't know how to find my way back home.

At that moment I was at peace and war with myself; what would happen next? What would this turn out to be? Nobody sets out to have a family and lose it. But I had to start with the facts. We had two beautiful children who needed both their parents. I thanked God that we were both reasonable people who, beneath it all, still loved one another enough to try and figure things out.

It didn't help any that I was between jobs. But if I could have chosen my circumstances, I'd rather be living in truth and broke than wealthy and miserable. And by that point truth was what we needed the most. Surprisingly, over time Jenn was doing better. I think the fact that I named my problem was a good thing in her mind.

So we began this journey of living the best we could while dealing with the emotional roller-coaster called marriage. When there are babies running around and growing up, it's hard to even recall what your life was about. That's kind of how we ended up in that circumstance in the first place...we forgot about us.

But one thing was clear, I wasn't giving up because I didn't want my kids to have part-time parents. I recall the scene in the *Godfather III* when the priest asked Michael Corleone when was the last time he had confession; and Michael replied that he had done too much (killing and such) to be forgiven. And the priest replied, "I heard you were a practical man...what do you have to lose?" That's where I was...just trying to be practical. But truthfully, your circumstances are only as real as how you clearly define them. And in that moment of hurt and anger, my inner situation looked bleak and felt even worse. Little did I know that things would feel and get worse really soon.

The search for a job and my sanity was taking a toll on me and my family. I had a little cash in the bank but I knew sooner than later that the cash would run out and we would be a full-time one-income household. I had to make something happen. But during this time I had moments where I was able to be by myself, with myself.

Let me explain. There are times when we feel lonely or sad and we yearn to be with others to be happy. It's in these moments that we actually can take advantage of being in the moment with ourselves; the moment of loneliness, or sadness, or even fear. Author and Buddhist nun Pema Chodron speaks about a place of *cool emptiness*. This is a place where we can process rather than avoid the realities that are happening within us. I was in that space. And something in me triggered a sense of opportunity. Now, this was well before I was introduced to Chodron's teachings. But this should resonate with each of us. We all have this inner something that at some point speaks truth to us. The question is *do we take it seriously and listen or do we shun it and disregard the moment.*

I listened to that voice; the voice to live in that moment of cool emptiness, to take in all of what was happening, why it happened, and how I wanted to learn from it and increase myself in the process. Chodron's latest book, "Welcoming the Unwelcome" is a book that goes deeper into many Buddhist teachings as this - I recommend reading her book once you're done here.

In my moments of despair, I was able to feel the pain of this real moment. So I did what I could do; I relaxed, took some deep breathes every day, and allowed myself to go through the steps of cool emptiness. I began to get more present with myself. I started thinking clearer and processing more about what I could do next - what I wanted to do next. Be mindful, this was happening for me in slow motion. Things around me were still in chaos but I was growing in a direction that would ultimately benefit everyone connected to me.

I was taking time for me because I was going through so much. I had been moving so fast with work, real estate investing, and just life, that I had not stopped to think and ask myself, "What am I doing all of this for?" I didn't know why I was doing what I was doing? Chodron reflects in her book, that asking this one simple question is paramount in a journey of connectedness..."Does this matter?" I hadn't asked myself that ever...and it would take another few years to understand that question.

At the time, I did understand that I was moving faster than I could see in front of myself. And I needed to be still - in gratitude. So I set a daily plan for myself to get more still. And I don't mean literally still. I would go swimming at the YMCA or work out in the gym. I would even go to get a massage or have lunch by myself. This is the stillness that involves cutting out the busy work in your head and getting present with what you are and where you are in life.

All of these activities were contrary to my normal drunken escapes that I had abused for so many years. I was becoming more conscious that being drunk in a club wasn't doing me any favors; and it wasn't going to help my marriage. I was leveling out my mind, my thoughts, and ultimately my behavior. It wasn't at all perfect but it was a start and I needed a start. These were times in which I was getting something I needed, but I was fighting it and still conflicted within my own self-awareness.

By this time Jen and I were doing the best we could considering the circumstances. She was experiencing things that I couldn't receive at that moment. It was selfish of me, but I didn't have the capacity; I was drained for so many reasons that I knew of and a ton of which I was searching to understand. It was like being a video game with prescribed movements and options, with each game ultimately concluding in a pre-determined conclusion. It wasn't perfect by any stretch, but it was us - and it was real.

For several years I attended the annual tennis US Open tournament in New York. I grew up a huge tennis fan, watching Agassi and Sampras knock each other around when I was a kid. I learned my backhand from watching Agassi on television and his bad-boy image resonated with me. So during my time of *cool emptiness* I was questioning if I should even attend the open since I was in-between jobs. But somewhere in my spirit, I convinced myself that I needed to get away, to continue processing, and New York in the summertime is a great place to process.

New York was amazing as usual. I visited the tennis center, took in some games, and just relaxed the entire time. I needed it more than I even initially thought. And NY delivered. While in NY Jen called me because some things at her job were up in limbo. It was a moment of clarity, being there for your spouse in a time of need when the reality was that you felt a million miles apart from one another. But what could I do? I had never been in this type of situation. I hadn't been married before and simultaneously experiencing personal brokenness. This was new terrain for Jen and I. I remember being in downtown Brooklyn when she called me and sitting down near a fountain.

The streets were crazy busy and loud and people were moving about, but at that moment it seemed as though I was the only one on the street. The hurt coming through the phone was that of a friend, not a distant spouse. And I just listened. Ironically, it was the first time in some years that I had felt that real genuine emotional connection in my marriage. And that was an amazing gift.

On the plane ride back, I sat down in the exit row with my earphones and phone ready to play my tunes so I would not be disturbed. But shortly into the flight, the guy next to me says something that always catches my attention..."Hey, that's a nice shirt you have on there, where'd you get it from?" He was referencing the fraternity shirt that I was wearing, and typically when someone asks you that, they are more than likely a brother of the same fraternity.

As people know me, I am all in for finding out if you are a brother of Omega Psi Phi. And indeed he was my fraternity brother. But even better, he was my older chapter brother which had an even deeper meaning. It meant that he knew the people that pledged me, and I surely knew the people that he pledged.

So I chucked the earphones and we talked the entire flight. We mostly discussed work. I walked him through my time as a grad student working overseas, all the way up to current day. By the time the plane had landed, we were back home. He was even gracious enough to invite me to play golf; and by the way, he said, "Shoot me your resume, we may have something for you where I work." Again, it seemed cool to me, but I didn't think much about the job opportunity. I just figured it was cool to meet a fellow chapter brother, and maybe he can help me think through my next move. Oh, and playing a round of golf never hurt anyone, ever!

Once back at home we eventually connected and we were able to play golf. It was cool to spend time with another black male who had his head on straight. He was a few years my senior and had already seen and done most of what I was experiencing. So our conversation was very fluid and unforced. As we played golf and talked about life, family, and work, I was in a good place. It was kind of strange, but I see clearly why that moment meant so much to me. Going back to my time at the Charlotte nonprofit, I began to realize that being around black men who I could look up to made me proud. It made me feel connected.

It was at that moment, on the golf course, that it hit me. My entire life I had been measuring black men in my life to that of a father figure. I was searching, seeking, and trying to connect with those black men that resembled what I longed for. I had not yet reconciled that my dad was who he was, and though not always physically present, he was still my dad. I had been searching all this time for connection, for affirmation, and a father's love.

How could a game of golf be so transformational? But it was. I felt a multiple emotions, from hurt to anger, to peace. All this time that had gone by when I acted out of frustration and hurt; I was pushing my feelings into a deep dark place where they could continue to live and present themselves in moments when I was too weak to open up honestly, or speak of my pain, and too ashamed to say exactly what I was searching for from my dad.

After playing a round of golf I had a life awakening experience. But for what it was worth, our chance meeting on that airplane had just ignited in me a growth point that would soon light a fire in me I never saw coming. Shortly after our golf outing, we discussed how I could fit into his company's team. I had previous experience in government public safety and his team sold public safety software. It just made sense that we would eventually work together. After accepting a job on his team, I went to work.

It was a great opportunity for me to jump right back into what I had started while at *Big Red*. I was able to meet customers and connect with them, learn about them, and understand how I could help them. This was my lane. I was feeling, more than ever before, that I had a boss that trusted me and an environment that allowed me to be me. As my family resettled in Charlotte, NC, I was feeling pure gratitude. We had more than most and we were doing well until what seemed to be a routine doctor's appointment for my wife became something more serious.

After having two children Jen could have claimed plenty of ailments, but she rarely did. The experience of having one child can be overwhelming, but having kids back to back (within fifteen months) is an entirely unique experience. At the time I didn't know exactly what she was going through, and I didn't have the empathy and compassion that I should have had. I failed big time and in hindsight, I can honestly say that I wasn't as present as I needed to be. I was so involved with me that I missed what was happening with Jen. It was as if we were living in two distinctly different lives.

Soon after getting settled into our new city Jen was having some follow-up medical appointments. They suggested to her that she get a check-up as a precaution. Initially, I don't think either of us thought much of it. But as time grew nearer our minds started to race a little more. But my heart was growing heavier by the day. The appointment to see what was going on with Jen came upon us pretty quickly, and it would turn out that Jen would need surgery.

Jen ultimately had the surgery and I began to look at my self-pity and frustrations as a distant memory. Because at that moment I became officially scared. What would happen to our family? How would our kids survive their mom not being around? How would I move on in life? All the questions were endless and I couldn't process any of them. I was freaking out and at the same moment, I felt something more powerful than I had ever felt before. In that moment of fear and confusion, I did what I knew would bring me the peace I needed - I became still again - in gratitude.

It was super transformative...there was no other alternative. I was overcome with a sense of gratitude. In all of the hurt and despair of a relationship that was holding on to dear life; with a wife that could at any moment be diagnosed with a disease that could turn your world up-side-down - I was just still and grateful.

I was grateful for the experiences and moments that we take for granted every single day of our lives. I began to remember just how we had reached that point where we were...I was grateful for changing my mind in high school and attending NC Central University instead of NC A & T because I met my wife while going to school in Durham. I was grateful for a mutual friend that thought Jen and I should connect and go out on a date. I became grateful for the dysfunction that forced me to leave my job and have time to move freely and spend time with Jen, so much that our relationship was deepened, and in five months we were engaged.

I was grateful for the two children that I never in my life imagined that I would be blessed with, and how beautiful they were and how I wouldn't want them to have had any other mother. I was grateful for the friendship that allowed us to figure out marriage without cutting each other down, and being reasonable and rationale in uncertainty.

But more importantly, I was grateful for the life that God had provided for me, for us. And in that moment of reflection, I began to understand the power of gratitude. No matter how bad it had gotten I had never felt so much gratitude in my life, and nothing else could exist in that space. Nothing else mattered but to feel the gratefulness of a life that was full of blessings.

I could push all the negative aside at that moment and focus on Jen; focus on what she needed, what our family needed. I was either going to check-in or get out. And I knew that I wanted to live life, not just be alive. I needed to check back in; our lives weren't what we wanted them to be, but they were all that God had scripted them to be. So we had to be obedient at that moment and walk through the storms.

Gratitude is a prickly thing. It can show you exactly how self-involved, selfish, and disconnected you really are. But the moment I realized that not addressing my internal stuff was keeping me from appreciating the blessings I had right in front of me, I stopped in my tracks. The storm that I felt coming made me stop, think, and drop to my knees in gratitude. I had missed out on so much and the way I viewed and lived my life would be forever changed.

Do you practice gratitude daily? Are you always asking for more or are you practicing gratitude for all that you have? Don't worry, if you are not there yet, you aren't alone. But I am 100% certain that if you just give it a try, your life will be transformed when you begin practicing gratitude...because it is more than an attitude, it's a lived experience.

I gratitude

Expression #6: I wake up every morning and I say, "Thank you." Why? Because I know that two things are for certain, 1) every day, someone is born into this world and 2) every day, someone is taken from this world. How often do you say thank you? How often do you find yourself thinking about how grateful you are, *because* of your circumstances? Yes, the type of gratitude that says thank you for the job lay-off, thank you for the years of personal grief and struggle, thank you for the financial obstacles that have drained my bank account. Thank you, because there would have been no blessings if there were never failures.

How often do you think about this level of gratitude? Not much? Why not? Is it because we can only be grateful for the good times and the good things we have in our lives? Or is it because we can't rationalize how being grateful for the times that make us uncomfortable, is the exact time we should have the most gratitude?

Gratitude is the starting point of experiencing a joyous life. Gratitude can't exist with despair, or anger, or even sadness. It exists on its own, by itself, because when we live in a place of gratitude our souls are full. *Answer the following question for yourself: How often does gratitude show up in your life 'because' of your circumstances (good and bad)?*

Gratitude Exercise

Expressions of gratitude have been proven to relieve stress, decrease anxiety levels, and create healthier human minds and bodies. This activity will challenge you to shift behaviors, incorporate new activities into your daily routine, and examine the differences that you see and feel in your life.

Instructions: For thirty (30) days, incorporate gratitude in your daily routine by incorporating the following three activities.

Morning Gratitude: When you wake up, speak out loud and write the three things that you are grateful for (they/it can be anything). The only rule is that you must speak and write new gratitude affirmations every morning. This activity starts your day off during, what I consider, the most important time of day, morning. This will allow you to program your heart and mind in positivity, affirming gratitude, *because* of what happened the previous day, or what is planned or unplanned for the current day. *Remember, language matters...so when we affirm gratitude 'because' of, we are affirming for ourselves in everything that happens in our life, good or bad, there is a reason to be grateful.*

Note: Gratitude - Lazarus and Lazarus (1994) argued "that gratitude is one of the 'empathic emotions' whose roots lie in the capacity to empathize with others...when you are grateful, it is impossible to also be hateful, angry, or fearful. Gratitude cannot be requested, demanded, or coerced, it can only be given. It is a gift, not an exchange.

Gratitude is a virtue because we chose to celebrate, rather than to resent, what is."

Mid-day Gratitude Meditation/Breathing: During the day, find fifteen (15) minutes to yourself and sit quietly, performing slow breathing, clearing your heart and mind of all thoughts and/or stressors; connecting with your state of being. The only rule is to be in the moment of calmness. This activity allows you to just be while releasing any anxiety, frustration, or negative feelings out of your physical and emotional state.

Note: Meditation - Multiple research studies have shown that meditation has the potential to decrease anxiety, thereby potentially boosting resilience and performance under stress (Seppala, 2015).

Daily Gratitude Journal: Writing in your gratitude journal can occur anytime during your day, but preferably when you have at least fifteen (15) to thirty (30) minutes of quiet time. You can write in a book, or do what I do, type in the notes section on a smartphone. The only rule is, there are none. Just write about anything you are feeling, and include what you are grateful for while reflecting and writing about your day. This activity is a therapeutic way of getting the thoughts in your head down on paper; so you can now have more clarity to embrace a new day, knowing that you can revisit what you have written if you so desire.

Note: Journaling - multiple studies have demonstrated the positive benefits of expressive writing in domains such as...

well-being. The findings indicate...fewer doctor visits and depressive symptoms, enhanced immune system...a host of other positive outcomes (Lepore & Smyth, 2002, and Smyth, 1998).

When you have finished*: If you missed some days, it's ok. Remember that practicing gratitude is not a race to the finish line; just continue to practice gratitude daily and find new ways that connect with you personally. After completing the exercise and practicing gratitude for thirty (30) days, spend some time reflecting on your behavior (emotions) during this period. How did the activities make you feel after they were completed each day? What aspects of your life did you see meaningful changes? How do you view yourself now and how do you view your life differently? What new habits will you incorporate into your life now?*

NOTES:

_____

_____

_____

_____

_____

_____

_____

_____

_____

_____

_____

_____

_____

_____

_____

_____

_____

_____

_____

_____

_____

_____

_____

7

MINDSET

I Attitude Shift I

If you can identify the process of empowering your mind, you can achieve anything you dream of and more.

. . . .

There was so much that was happening all at once in my life. Kids, wife, job; I was living the life of so many other people, yet it felt like I was the only one. But I knew better, what I was experiencing was nothing special. I was up and down, back and forth, and all over the place with my emotions. They had gotten the best of me and I didn't have control over them. I had always prided myself on being highly self-aware, but I couldn't see clearly about what was real. I was so self-involved that I had lost myself.

After a few weeks of waiting, we found out that Jen was healthy and cleared to live her life. Listen, I don't care how much pain and anger you are going through personally. You have to know, at that moment, I felt like a whole new man. It was a moment that is indescribable...when you think about what could have happened as opposed to what just actually happened. You feel so grateful while you cringe at the thought of how you could have been so selfish. It wasn't my proudest moment - but God. It was a wake-up call for me to deal with my stuff while being grateful that I had stuff to deal with. Life is a gift and I needed to intentionally and passionately enjoy it.

Don't get me wrong, I was far from being in a great place, but there's nothing that says you have a new lease on life like the news of a healthy family. We were in a blessed state and in those moments we were grateful. There are times in your life when it feels as though you are just existing in time and space. During this time in my life, I was grappling with this existence. I was back on the road traveling for my job, but still trying to figure out where I was emotionally, mentally, and spiritually. I wasn't broken, but I was lost. And being lost can be the most difficult existence in life.

My job at the time was to travel and meet with customers to ensure they were happy with our company's services. It was a great opportunity for me to stay connected with people, to just continue to develop relationships that were meaningful in some manner. The travel also allowed me to decompress in a safe and healthy way. In earlier years, I tended to drown much of my pain in alcohol, drugs, and strip clubs, so the traveling was a far better outlet.

While traveling, I was still developing my ideas of how I could continue to speak to organizations about my thoughts on leadership. While at *Big Red* I was able to travel to visit universities and speak to students of color who were interested in retail careers. It allowed me to tap back into what I was good at - connecting and inspiring people.

In middle school, I was asked if I would like to speak for a school event. I was in seventh-grade at the time and one of the English teachers was in charge of this event. I was excited and recall being nervous, but not so nervous as to pass the opportunity up. The event was a sort of speech contest and I don't even know if I won or lost. I just remember that I felt so comfortable speaking in front of people about something I was passionate about.

Ultimately, for our eighth-grade graduation, I was asked to give a speech for the *graduation charge*. This was a speech about moving on from middle school to high school, and it was a great privilege for me. As I walked up to the microphone, I remember hoping that no one would notice my very weird walking. My shoes were so tight that I could barely move in them and I was so embarrassed, but I walked with my head held high. I gave my speech, the audience applauded, and at that moment I had caught the *inspiration* bug.

In high school, I would go on to participate in more speaking engagements, and I was active in band and eventually took up playing tennis. But I always enjoyed speaking. I was selected as one of our band's drum majors in twelfth-grade. It was a huge deal to be a drum major, especially in Atlanta where bands were the culture. My role as a drum major was to lead by example, to direct, and to keep the order of this massive sound machine. I was in heaven.

I had arrived at being drum major through some personally difficult times growing up. I was a fairly good kid but I had a lot of hurt inside me so I acted out quite a bit; mostly through arguing and fighting. And I was pretty small so I believed in hitting when I felt threatened. My mom would eventually share with me a poem by Charles Swindoll entitled *Attitude*. It was an excerpt actually from an original literature piece. But the poem was very relevant for me and it reshaped how I viewed myself. I kept the original paper that my mom gave me the poem on.

That was over thirty years ago. My attitude was at the core of what was helping me and hurting me at the same time. Even at the young age of eleven, I couldn't see clear to get out of my own way. Yes, that's probably par for the course at that age, but I was conscious enough to know that if my attitude wouldn't shift, my life would be a long and difficult road. The poem had a line that to this day I recite for myself, "Life is 10% what happens to you, and 90% of how you respond."

As I grew up and out into the world, the realization of just how much one's attitude was key to living a joyous life, became very evident to me. As I continued searching for a greater purpose in life, more meaning in my life, I began reflecting on my thoughts and feelings. I started to look inward and began assessing me, my energy, my vibe; what was I portraying to the world around me?

All these questions were making me think and feel deeper about where I had come from; not so much anymore what had happened, but how did I really feel about it and what did that mean to me. Panache Desai, the self-described *old friend*, says that the key to finding yourself is through acceptance of self. I was experiencing a journey of acceptance. While I was so focused on suppressing and leaving behind my pain, I hadn't realized that I never had allowed myself to truly feel the pain. The hurt, the resentment, all of it had built up inside of me and weighed me down to a point that I couldn't move. I couldn't see the purpose in my life because I couldn't feel real emotions. I was having a moment of clarity.

My entire life I had been moving through halls of escapism, repressing, denying; rejecting positives and negatives. That was my strategy to be strong for me; to be able to push through. I could conquer any trial as long as I kept my feelings and the reality of the moment separate. "Stop being sensitive," my mom would tell me growing up. I took it to heart and I became a *tough guy*.

But as I came into my own as a young adult, my relationships began to reflect some very obvious defects in my emotional capacity to connect with others on a heart-centered level; a truly authentic space. The only time where I felt I was truly free, fully myself, was when I was speaking in front of an audience. There was something about standing in front of people who wanted to hear the words from your heart, come through your voice. It felt real to me, like a responsibility that was unlike any other. I recall my college student affairs dean, Dr. Roger Bryant (God rest his super soul), sharing words of encouragement after I had given a student government speech while running for freshman class president...he said, "Glenn, you have a gift to inspire people...never lose it." His words meant everything to me, but at the time, it was less what he said and more how he said it. I remember vividly the look in his eyes as she shook my hand. It was as if he saw something in me, something that I clearly didn't see yet.   All I knew was that when I spoke I was speaking form my hurt, my heart, my passion.

After finding out Jen was going to be ok, my life was being filled with moments of acceptance. I was experiencing thirty plus years of feeling my emotions and accepting them for all of what they meant to me. As I paced myself on this journey I began to see more clearly. I started to focus on what life meant to me, what I meant to this world, and how I wanted to show up every single day. And the clarity in my life began to be revealed. I began to see God's blessings working in overdrive. I started to understand that if I wanted my life to work, my marriage to work - I would have to put work into it.

After working with the company for a little over two years I had come to a point that I needed to move on. My friend had left the company and I knew that my time there would be coming to an end soon.   I was feeling more connected to myself and the experiences that I wanted to have in life were becoming clearer.

I landed a job as Executive Director for a nonprofit serving kids, helping them develop as students, and supporting their behavior development.   When I interviewed for the job I had the opportunity to meet with my direct reports. They were three women who had a passion for the work and the team. As I spoke to them, I felt a connection with them. They were there because they were connected to the mission. And I was there because I was connected to the same thing. Before I entered the room, I had made up my mind to not take the job if offered. But after sitting with them and sharing that experience with them, a scheduled fifteen-minute conversation turned into more than thirty-minutes of human connection.

I was sold. If offered the job I would have to commute 2.5 hours to work (my home was in Charlotte, and the job was in Rocky Mount, NC), but I didn't care. There was something about these women that touched me and resonated with me. So I jumped in head first and it was one of the best decisions I have ever made.

As I commuted from Charlotte to Rocky Mount, I would take that time to think about how I wanted to continue developing learning experiences for leaders...what issues were important, what types of sessions would I create, what types of experiential exercises would help people become better people - better leaders. Since my time at *Big Red*, I had started a routine of writing things down. Before then, I rarely ever would write thoughts or ideas down. I would have conversations with people or speak in public, and people would always ask me, "Do you have that written somewhere?" If I had a dollar...well, you know the rest. So I made it a point to begin writing; because if I was going to achieve greater heights, I had to shift my thinking - elevate my mindset.

The iPhone was my greatest tool for writing. I began writing all my ideas, thoughts, and experiences that meant anything to me, in the notes section of my phone. Initially, I found it kind of weird and sometimes worrisome. But I stayed with it and I began to see that I was thinking clearer and able to process better because I had written things down. I started to love writing again...back in middle school is when I truly enjoyed it; I had now come to a place in life where writing was fun and exciting again.

While commuting, thinking, and processing, I was able to think of some great ideas and my writing began to evolve. Abstract thoughts started to connect and make me think deeper. One day while driving to lunch in Rocky Mount I had a scheduled call with a hospital administrator about facilitating a leadership class. She had been referred to me by a mutual colleague who I had performed some work for years prior. For a few minutes we talked shop and exchanged pleasantries, and the call ended fairly quickly without any fanfare. I thought that I would be getting some type of request to perform some work but it didn't happen. I chalked it up for what it was and I tried to keep a positive mindset.

Later that same night I was staying in a Rocky Mount hotel, and I ended up waking up early in the morning because I had been tossing and turning all night. I got up and started writing. I had some thoughts about learning session ideas and I had to write them down before I forgot them. After I finished showering, I checked my email and there it was; an email from the executive I had spoken to earlier that day. She had sent the email at 4:30 AM. It was a simple email; she wanted to know if I could facilitate a session on a specific topic and send her the outline ASAP. I immediately knew what to send her. I started writing the email and I pressed send. Shortly after, I was thinking to myself - that wasn't it. When I was in the shower earlier that morning I had a thought about another idea, but I wasn't sure it would go over well. It was an idea that I believed in, but it was very outside of the box, and I didn't want to blow my chance.

But in my heart, I knew that topic was it. That's what she needed, and I needed to be courageous enough to put it out there and live with the outcome. By this time over an hour had gone by and she had not replied to the first email I sent. I wasn't sure if sending another email would seem desperate or unprofessional, but I was over-thinking it. I decided to send the session topic that I believed would be the one. I typed it out, took a deep breath, and pressed send one last time. Within five minutes she replied, "That's it!" Wow...that was it; the one topic that I was the most passionate about, and the most fearful of sharing was the topic that received the quickest response. The session topic was entitled *love in logic.*

When you are in the midst of something big, the reality is, your gut tells you but your mindset compels you. I was about to be out of luck if I allowed my mindset to think safe. This was a moment that I needed to be authentic, gutsy, and courageous. I was so scared in that moment to share what I passionately believed in, that I could have missed what turned out to be a major growth moment in my life.

After hearing that my *love in logic* topic was the direction that we would take for the upcoming training session, I began to believe. I know it may sound weird, but don't get it confused. We all have times when we aren't strong; we have a hard time believing because all of what we see is so blurry. I had started truly believing and realizing that God has placed a gift in me that couldn't be quantified by money or gigs booked. It was a gift that I had never fully appreciated and if I wanted to live the life that God meant for me to live, I would have to speak life into my purpose. I needed an attitude shift.

So I decided that I needed to get serious about the business of cultivating and honing my craft. I had to begin to synthesize my many thoughts and ideas to craft theories, test, and develop them. I was ready to begin taking all those experiences and blessings along the way and transform them into works of service. This was my door and I had to knock it down. The training session that I would be preparing for was taking place about three months out. Meanwhile, I was steadily driving back and forth to work, commuting the long haul because I loved my team and I was there for a reason. You see, the *love in logic* topic came from an experience while working with my Rocky Mount team.

The main job of our team was to work with children in schools to help them with either academics, behavior, or other challenges they may be facing as students. And part of my role as executive director was to identify opportunities where our teams could have greater impact in the lives of the children we served, in and out of school.

One day while visiting with one of our school leaders I was observing the interactions between a student and a facilitator. It dawned on me that something was missing in their conversation. As I sat and watched, I could see that the facilitator was trying her best to get across her point to the student. While on the other hand, the student was not responding well to her attempts.

This went on for about thirty minutes and nothing changed. Afterward, we allowed the students to leave the room and we sat there to discuss what had just transpired. I asked her, "How do you feel that went?" And she replied with a shrug, "Ok, I guess." She continued to share how there is little motivation in many of the students because of a variety of reasons; mostly because they just don't trust adults or have just given up.

At that moment, I felt my heart smile. I felt warm inside because I knew what she was talking about. I had experienced that feeling before; as a child and as an adult. But I also knew there was a way that she could turn that feeling around for those students. I took a deep breath and asked her, "Have you ever tried just talking to the students without responding to their complaints...just listening and maybe even sharing some of your stories with them?"

You see, the interactions between them were void of something very important - love. There was an obvious absence of *love* in their communication. And as Rick Warren says, "Leadership without love is manipulation." She paused and sat silent for a few seconds. I could see her mind twisting and turning. I interjected in the silence and continued with saying, "There seems to be an absence of love in your logical conversation...and because there is no selfless, genuine, and unconditional love, the student is unable to be vulnerable, or open, or even fully present." She smiled. It was making sense to her, and I could see that the wheels that were turning for her were the same wheels that had been turning for me while I was at *Big Red*.

My long-awaited *ah-hah* moment had happened for me. I was living in real-time the unfolding of what my purpose in life was, and each day I saw it clearer. My voice was being used to share my experiences, my pain, my reflections, my vulnerability. And to fully receive God's calling on my life I would have to continue to be present with the emotions of my heart. I would continue on a journey that could only be defined as heart work.

When you carry around a fixed mindset you are effectively fighting yourself. Yes, we all think about *what if* when it comes to the important things in our life, especially our careers and families. But if you invested your energy into what you are passionate about, and not your *plan B*, your outcomes would be drastically different. *Well, what happens when my plan A fails Glenn?* If you are determined and believe in what you want out of life, then pick up those pieces and find another way. What I have learned from all of these gutsy moments was that I was so busy worrying about what wouldn't work (and what didn't work), I wasn't spending time on what I wanted to work. See the difference...I was opting out of everything that wasn't easy - including my marriage. Why? Because I had a *plan B*.

My attitude was not constructed with a *plan-A-only* growth mindset; an attitude that challenged me to put in the necessary work so that I could achieve my audacious goals in life. So I had to check myself, check my mindset and choose to shift my attitude to receive the blessings that were right in front of me. Now, ask yourself, what type of mindset are you leading with?

I mindset

Expression #7: The human mind is a powerful tool; often described as the most powerful organism that exists. And mindset can be best described as a person's attitude, mental state, and set of beliefs. My mother told me when I was a child, "There's nothing you can't do in life as long as you put your mind to it." These words ring truer each day I draw breath. When I was younger, the popular saying was *a mind is a terrible thing to waste.* And in fact, that is a pop culture campaign that has never been debated.

The most powerful challenge we experience is constructing our mindset - our attitude about what's happening within us, and right in front of us. It's the difference between asking what is happening to me, or leveling up and asking what am I learning from this? When you can learn from your life experiences, you can leverage your gifts and skills to be great.

Mindset is everything! If your mind is not yours, so goes your life. Yes, it's that serious. If you can identify the process of empowering your mind, you can achieve anything you dream of and more. As you assess where you are in life and where you want to be, do you have the right attitude to help power you towards your destination? *Answer the following question for yourself: How will you shape your mindset to leverage your inherent greatness?*

Mindset Exercise

A fixed mindset undoubtedly creates in a person limiting beliefs and a limited mind, creating in them an inability to learn and grow. Alternatively, a growth mindset is cultivating, nurturing, and fosters an optimistic attitude for one's personal development.

Instructions: In this exercise, examine and develop your growth mindset. First, detail what happened in your most recent and/or most impactful failure moment(s) in your personal or professional life, then answer the following questions:

Q1: How did it make me feel?

Q2: What did I learn?

Q3: What are some growth strategies that I can develop from this?

Q4: Who could I help with what I have learned?

Q5: How will this influence my mindset moving forward?

As you complete the exercise, think about what your mindset reflects now and what you want it to reflect moving forward. Now, write down your mindset mantra: This is an affirmation statement that explicitly states how you view yourself, obstacles, life overall, and the lens in which you will use to envision your future.

(Ex: I am a strong-willed father and committed husband; I see failure as fuel, and I know that life is meant to be lived and I choose to live it to its fullest.)

NOTES:

_____

_____

_____

_____

_____

_____

_____

_____

_____

_____

_____

8

GREATNESS

I Your Move I

Average is taught. Greatness is earned.

. . . .

Steve Farber, author of "Radical Leap" says to fully embrace extreme leadership, you must ultimately show proof. When I read his book in 2005 I was in the middle of my leadership whirlwind storm and I needed some life support, to say the least. A new friend saw that I was going through some things, and after a conference that we were attending ended, I arrived back home to a copy of Farber's critically acclaimed book in my mailbox.

- The book "Radical Leap" changed my life. Thanks Steve.

After receiving the opportunity to deepen my experience with organizational clients, I began to look at my work differently. Not that I didn't know what I was good at, but I didn't know how my work would take shape. I had never thought about how I would show *proof*. I knew that in order to translate my opportunities into greater experiences I would have to rethink and redesign my work mindset, and then I would have to show proof.

For five years I did not make one single cent from the training, speaking engagements, or coaching that I had led; Not ONE penny. So in preparation for my first paid speaking engagement, I had to mentally tap into what this growth moment meant to me. Would it mean that I had arrived? Did it mean that I could slow down a bit and relax? Did it even mean that I could now start thinking about how much money I was going to make?

But after deep reflection and personal analysis, what I realized was that moment meant so much more about something totally different. In those moments of exhilaration and excitement, I knew the opportunity meant I would have to work smarter, dig deeper, and have greater focus. It was time for me to become a student of my craft, a learner, a researcher, a scholar.

Up until that point, I had relied heavily on my practitioner knowledge and experiences. I had begun writing and researching but I was not reading as I should. I mean the kind of reading where you set aside a few hours in the day to solely be in tune with some form of literature. This epiphany came to me while processing this blessed experience that I had been praying about for so long.

I began dissecting everything that I did and didn't do during the day. From my sleep habits to scheduling daily tasks, even to how often and what I was eating. This was the first time in my adult life that I was laser-focused on developing habits that would exponentially increase my ability to be more than just successful...I wanted greatness.

When standing in front of leaders, or whatever you choose to do in life, the one goal you should have is to leave it/them better off than when you entered. That's my goal every single time I open my mouth to an audience. I want to ensure that no matter who is in the room - if they are willing participants, will leave in better condition, more empowered, more knowledgeable, more focused, and more understanding of what it takes to achieve the goals they have set for themselves.

But this decision to rethink how I prepared myself to activate my God-given gift meant loving myself in a way I had never done before. It meant taking what I had uncovered in my heart, the pain and anger, and all the things I had pushed away, and going to the place of full acceptance. This isn't an easy step for most people. But if you are willing to embrace doing things that make you uncomfortable there are no heights that you can't reach. It's the discomfort that lets you know that you are expanding, that you are shifting in mindset, and what must follow are your behaviors and habits.

Eric Thomas, the acclaimed motivational speaker, shares insights about how one must honor, hone, and cultivate their craft. As the time drew near for my training session, people would ask me if I was prepared. And almost

149

always I would answer that question with a resounding yes. But this time was different; there was so much more on the line and I had never been in a position where I felt as though I wasn't prepared. I began thinking about all the years before that day. Had I honored my craft fully? Had I taken the time to spend time with more content, research, and other leaders in the field? Had I spent too much time on leisure travel before putting in the time with purpose work?

It wasn't a moment of second-guessing...it was a moment of harsh clarity and harsher reality. Yes, I would be ready to deliver once the day came but would I be ready for the next time, and the time after that when the stakes would be higher and greater. I was coming into my own understanding of just how important it is to hone one's craft...not for the short-term outcome, but for the expectation of greatness.

There was no denying that I was in my moment of acknowledging my story, accepting me for me, and aligning my blessed experiences with purpose in my life. I was feeling, seeing, and hearing differently. My senses were on high alert and all around me, the elements had changed. I was experiencing a place of intention and deliberateness like never before. I was sinking up to a higher calling and my mindset was flushing out the destructive, stagnant, useless information in my spirit and opening up my determination and hunger. It was time for me to make my move.

Are you aware of what makes one inherently great?
I am. It's everything from one's natural skills and gifts, to their quirky personality traits and silly weirdness. Deep inside

every living human being is a seed of inherent greatness. Some of us water that seed and some of us choose otherwise. Are you watering your greatness? Or are you feeding yourself false narratives that are deterring you from living your life to the fullest? It's time, if you haven't yet, to step right into all that you were created to be. The story that we all should tell ourselves is the one that starts with *I was created inherently great, and I am going to live out loud that greatness in all that I do.*

For much of my life, as far back as I can remember, I have always been able to see my reality. And my ability to be self-aware was typically high. But trying to make real-life changes takes more than self-awareness; it takes some intensive, targeted, focused work. For me, it took the form of working on three areas of my life; my heart, my mind, and my body. I knew that for me to fully receive what God had planned for my life, I would have to love myself by showing proof of what I was willing to do to step into my purpose.

Medical researchers have long studied the effects of our physical wellness on our mental and heart health. So for me, I needed to pay more attention to what was transpiring within me and my body. Yes, I worked out and was in pretty good shape. But the food I put in my body, the alcohol I had been abusing since my teenage years, and the marijuana I had consumed for more than 30 years surely were not positively contributing to my purpose in life. To paraphrase Cicely Tyson...*when I put my head on my pillow at night, I don't require alcohol, a drug, or anything - just fatigue.* This is the life I wanted to live.

By ignoring my physical wellness I was cheating God, my clients, and more importantly myself. I wasn't able to fully be present when I needed to be. I was operating on limited capacity because I had always been able to get by and do just enough. But when greatness is your goal, you can't cheat the process. Greatness requires all of you times ten, and that is what I wanted in my life. I was in a place of willingness and desire, so much so that the drugs and alcohol, the leisure time, the menial things that I had once relished no longer had relevance. I had to take back control.

My diet, what I placed in my mouth, mattered to me now. My energy level mattered to me and to be 110 percent for myself, my family, and my clients, I had to be present and accounted for. There was no more room for being tipsy and high; time and energy would not allow for it. There was no more room for food that disrupted my guts; my body needed to function on a high level to fulfill my service to others through my craft. I made this commitment to myself because I had to be able to demonstrate a discipline for my life, to inspire others to be courageous enough to do so themselves.

While working on my body, I also knew that I had neglected my mind for far too long. The time spent on mindless entries into my brain was exhausting. The withdrawals that I had allowed to happen day in and day out, while not replenishing my mind with nourishment and enrichment had taken a toll on me. I would have to ask myself a question, "What substantive experience can I truly bring forth to others if I can't even fill my tank?"

I had been doing just enough because for those seasons just enough was getting me through. But again, greatness would require far more than I had ever given to myself or any other person. Greatness was requiring me to re-focus on me; because my purpose needed a greater investment from me.

When I decided to choose to invest in my psychological wellness, my outlook shifted, my energy was renewed, and I sensed a calmness in my being. It was as if I had been reborn with new super-powers and all I needed to do was nurture them. I began to practice yoga and breathing, taking, walks, and reading. No more alcohol or drugs; just my drive to be what God created me to be.

Every day was a day of centeredness, being in the moment so my mind could receive what was happening at that moment. And when I would get distracted, I wouldn't fight it, I would allow the distraction to take place. Then I would calmly set it aside and move on. Trust me when I say that these shifts in my world were not easy - are not easy. But they are all possible. This process of working *inside-out* is about pure determination, desire, and will. Are you hungry enough? Do you truly desire greatness or are you simply talking a good game? For so many years I talked a great game. But my habits - my behavior, told a different story.

As I experienced the process of healing my body and my mind, I continued the journey of healing my heart. When I was younger I never stopped to think about the weights that I had inside of me. I had kept inside of me the weights of deeply rooted anger, hurt, and distrust. It was heavier than I ever realized and that's what is tricky about your heart. We push so much down inside of us, attempting to just move forward and not think about our feelings. But those emotions do not just magically disappear. They are still there, just repressed, and dormant in our sub-conscious; they appear in the most unexpected and untimely circumstances.

Heart Work is the title of this book for several reasons, but specifically because the work that I have been experiencing over the past thirty years can only be summed up into those two words - heart work. It's the work that we shy away from the most. If I were to ask a group of people (men and women) if they would prefer to do hard work or heart work, I am quite sure that hard work would be an overwhelming selection.

Well, why is that? Why is heart work so difficult? For me, and so many other people, my journey in heart work started as a journey in trials and tribulations. I didn't know I was working on my heart; all I knew was that I was going through the ringer and each time something triggered me I would go into a place of deep reflection and contemplation. It wasn't until I began to be present with my thoughts and emotions that I was able to determine that I was intentionally working on my heart. I was working on processing my life experiences for what they were. I was shedding my self-pity, blame, and anger, and acknowledging that it happened and it was real. And it may not have always been ok, but I was ok and better for it.

It was time for me to take my story and use it for what God had built me for. My story is a guide for someone, especially someone like me. Each of us has a survival guide story. And when we decide to acknowledge it, accept it, and align it for the greater good of others, it becomes the super-power that you deep down knew you had. So what are you willing to do to be great? Not the selfish "greatness," no, I am speaking of the selfless greatness. The you who forgives and inspires others to be their best version of themselves. Heart-centered leaders lead from a place of love, compassion, and service - this is what we call greatness.

One of the most asked questions I receive from kids and adults is how do you get over people doubting you and self-doubt? And there is only one answer; you must believe in yourself more than the desire for others to believe in you. I realized early on in life that even my most avid supporter will eventually have doubts about my ability to achieve goals I have set for myself. And when you come to understand that another human being will not, cannot, and should not believe in your journey more than you, you will be on the fast track to achieving your dreams.

Growing up I had a good number of champions, but no one was more instrumental in the development of my personal belief system than my mother. For all of our differences, there is one constant, she believed in me one thousand percent. It didn't matter what it was...baseball, trumpet, tennis, public speaking, or even running for mayor of Atlanta. Whatever I decided to try, she always would say, "You can do anything you put your mind to, and more." After hearing it so much as a youngster, it's almost impossible to not believe it yourself. So I grew up with this *belief DNA*, an attitude of audacity - that whatever I wanted to accomplish in life, I could do it.

But I would soon find out as an adult, that even my mother's belief in me had its limits. I recall when I decided to run for mayor of Atlanta; it was a moment of extreme belief in myself that I could do something I was sure no one would believe I could achieve. But for me, stretching myself has always been a way of life. My mother, on the other hand, was apprehensive. And it wasn't that she didn't believe in me, it was her mother's intuition that made her feel nervous for me. Politics has always been a polarizing endeavor in Atlanta, and she conveyed her hesitance very early on in my journey to run for office. Her fear for my well-being was prohibiting her to fully embrace my ambitious goal.

But we must understand this, our personal goals will not and should not be accepted by everyone around us including the people we love the most. Your vision is your vision, and the idea that someone else can be equally as excited, motivated, and committed to believing in it is simply not plausible. If you have a goal and it's so big that you are scared, then you best believe that you may just be out on that ledge by yourself. And being on that ledge by yourself is totally ok (and sometimes necessary)!

When I started to understand what I wanted to do with my life - what my blessed experiences meant to me and for me, I began to realize that this path I was on was not a lane that was over-crowded. In fact, the lane I had created was empty, it was me and my beliefs, my emotions, my thoughts, my passion. I was there by myself but there were whispers of encouragement and support all around me. The difference was that I had to decide - was I ready to travel in my own lane no matter the outcome? Was I ready to commit to what God had placed in me? I had to have a belief in my abundance, enormity, and greatness.

I chose to be self-aware enough, conscious enough, to be real with myself and those around me. I had to acknowledge the frustrations that would come with people not seeing what I could see, believing in what I knew was right, or lifting me when I needed to be lifted. I needed to be aware that these frustrations would occur and I would have to be honest enough with myself to know that what I was feeling was not anyone's fault but my own. The people around me had only one job and that was to be themselves. That's it, I couldn't expect them to be my cheerleading section, my respite, or my shoulder to cry on. I had to know that this path I had chosen was a path unknown to them. And if I wanted them to learn about my path and its meaning, I would have to have enough belief in myself to create such a compelling demonstration of purpose that they would eagerly choose to join me.

I always say to myself that hungry people find a way to eat. And I wanted to eat! Will Smith (*The Fresh Prince of Bel-Air*) says that on the other side of fear is greatness. If you are willing to do the real work and focus, life will reveal itself to you in ways that seem unimaginable.

This is the road to greatness. A well-traveled journey is far better than a tantalizing destination - making your move, working *inside-out*, and believing in yourself like no one else can. Do you want to be great? Do the heart work - the necessary work. This is my lane that I choose to live in. I could have easily selected another direction or course of action; but when you do your heart work, when you get real with you, it becomes increasingly difficult to look yourself in the mirror and settle for good - when you know you were created inherently great.

I greatness

Expression #8: Greatness can be best described as the moment when your gifts meet your will. If you look around the world - the evolution of the human experience, you can easily conclude that greatness lives in each of us. The question is, however, are you willing to do what it takes to unleash your greatness? College coach and former Duke basketball star Jeff Capel puts it like this, "You have to fall in love with the process of becoming great." And that's just what it is, simple and plain. Your inherent greatness does not preclude you from WORK. Oh no; it's the total opposite. Your inherent greatness requires you to dig deeper, to do your heart work, and commit yourself to a life of gratitude, purpose, and love.

Were you the one that had so much potential growing up? Did you have dreams of being awesome at something that you were passionate about and would even do for free without a second thought? So, what happened? Did it happen? If not, why not?

Many of us start off in life with the hope in our eyes and fire in our belly and along the way something deters us. Life punches us in the gut and mouth and stops us in our tracks. And then our greatness turns to good, or worse, average. Ultimately, we become stuck. Stuck in a place that is ok, but just not good enough. Because you still remember what it felt like to have greatness in you. The only difference now is that you can't remember 'how' to unleash it anymore.

Unfortunately, this story is a common one. But there is a way out, a path forward. You just have to be willing, courageous, and determined enough to step into the greatness you have always had inside of you. In my life, I have known many people that wanted to unleash their greatness. But they didn't know where to start. *Average is taught. Greatness is earned.*

Answer the following question for yourself: What are you willing to do to unleash your greatness?

Greatness Exercise
It's past time for you to reveal your inner greatness. There may be something that has been inside you for all of your life. Or maybe there is something that recently happened to you that has you thinking, "I could do that...I want to do that." Whatever it is, I want you to take this opportunity to map out how you are going to activate what is inherent inside of you - *greatness.*

Instructions: In this exercise, you will write down what you are great at...not good, but great. And this can be a variety of things. What distinguishes you from the next person (not comparing, but acknowledging your gifts)? Are you extremely good at fixing things? Do you have a keen ability to empathize with others? Can you write well? Whatever your gift(s), this is your time to acknowledge it. After writing down what you're great at, answer the following questions to help guide you in mapping out how you will continue to "earn your inherent greatness."

Q1: *What are you great at? (Write up to three)*

Q2: *What have you done with this gift in your life?*

Q3: *Is this a gift that you truly believe in?*

Q4: *If nothing was stopping you, what would you do with your gift?*

Q5: *What is stopping you from living out your greatness in your gift?*

Now, commit to yourself the three habits you will consistently execute for the next 30 days to move closer to your inherent greatness (Ex.: I will wake up at 5 am every morning and exercise for 20 minutes. I will read for 60 minutes every Monday - Friday. And I will "start" today, without reservation, on outlining, planning, and acting on my gift).

As you complete this exercise, take notice of your responses and the habits you outlined for yourself. Are you committed to doing what it takes to unleash all that is great about you? Are you willing to step into a growth mindset and disregard the negativity and naysayers that may surround you? If so, then continue to write down how you will execute on behaviors and habits that will fuel your energy and inspiration to continue being great. And go earn what you deserve!

GO. BE. GREAT!!!

NOTES:

_____

_____

_____

_____

_____

_____

_____

_____

_____

_____

_____

_____

_____

_____

_____

9

JOY

I More meaning, greater joy I

When you have accepted you, just as you are, you actually have taken one more step...closer to joy.

Chasing money can blind your focus and disrupt your faith. As a young professional, I wanted to do just a few things, gain access, get promoted into greater roles, and earn more money. And there was nothing wrong with that, other than I didn't understand that achieving all three did not mean I would experience joy in my life.

Joy can seem as elusive as air; you know it exists, you know it's there, but you can't grab it. For as long as I can remember, the question for me has always been what is joy. Is it happiness? Or is it something different. I have come to understand that joy differs from happiness. Happiness is fleeting and is dependent on circumstances.

Joy, on the other hand, exists regardless of your situation. If you have joy in your heart, sadness may come but your joy is steadfast. Anger and conflict may occur but your joy will not fade. The reason is because joy is a state of being. Joy is the convergence where gratitude meets purpose, meets love - when your why, what, and how are aligned. And purpose is a key factor in how we experience joy in our lives.

Purpose is a very misunderstood word. Just like your story is important but doesn't define you, purpose is within you but isn't just one thing. Why? Well purpose, contrary to public opinion, is dynamic. Yes, purpose can change for you; it doesn't have to be a fixed proposition, it can evolve. My purpose in life when I was 16 years old is quite different than it is now. Every day in our lives we have a purpose. It could be to just go to work and learn a new skill so you can be prepared for a new opportunity. Your purpose could be to serve others through telling your personal story. Or your purpose could be manifested by being an at-home dad so you can spend quality time with your children. Whatever it may be, purpose is within you always, you just have to receive it.

Some people have a purpose that helps millions, and some have a purpose that may help just one. No matter what, your purpose in life is invaluable and meaningful and is exactly what it is supposed to be. When we say we *seek to find purpose*, I challenge the language we use in that thought process. I would change that statement to *I want to reveal my purpose*. In revealing your purpose you challenge yourself to think and feel deeply; you challenge yourself to perform the necessary heart work that ultimately reveals what is already present within you in that exact moment. You are looking to receive the purpose that your life is reflecting for you, through you.

Earlier in the book, I shared my feelings on gratitude. And now we can define how joy exists. When you can have gratitude and purpose, you are in a space of joy. For many years as a young adult, I struggled to truly understand joy. I went through the ups and downs of being temporarily happy one moment to utterly depressed the next. It was as if I was on a rollercoaster ride and I couldn't predict how I would respond to the unknown twists and turns.

But *having joy* is really about revealing *you*. Let me say it this way; you are joy. Remember the acceptance path? When you have accepted you, just as you are, you have taken one more step closer to you - closer to joy. These steps are all interrelated and if you can spend quality time with your thoughts and feelings, you become more equipped with the tools you need to discover you. That's the heart work.

As I ventured into my journey to teach, to stand before others and share my story, I came to a place of realization about my personal joy. I didn't have any. I didn't have the joy in my life that I wanted and deserved. I was plagued by my heart work deficiencies. And I knew that to fully embrace my purpose, I would have to first do the heart work that was resting in my spirit.

At first, I didn't know where to start. I had been experiencing life-changing moments and learning from so many things and people around me but I wasn't clear on where I would begin my work. So I decided to be still. Remember, when we are still we can go to a deeper place within ourselves that speaks to us truthfully. Some say that voice is God, some say it's the spirit of the Infinite. Whatever you believe, it is a place where you can hear the truth; where you can be present in a moment that requires your total commitment and attention. In that place, I was able to hear my truth and understand that for me to move forward I would need to start from within.

I began to practice gratitude and eventually outlined my purpose. That purpose statement is on my refrigerator and I see it every single day. But writing that statement out was a life-altering moment for me, my family, and every single person that I come into contact with. Why? Because when I wrote that statement out, plain and simple as it is, I activated my gift - the joy inside me. I was all in and there was nothing that would stop me from being all that God created me to be. That's when I decided I was willing to do what it took to be great. A pretty famous book entitled *The Holy Bible* says, "A man's gift makes room for him" (Proverbs 18:16).

At the age of twenty-eight, I was earning $69k. By the time I turned 35, I was earning more than $125k a year. I should have been the happiest person in the world. I could afford everything I wanted. I was living the so-called American dream. But there was one thing not right. I had no personal joy. Yes, my family brought me joy, my work to some degree brought me joy. But absent those things, I wasn't personally filled with joy. I was empty, living off of warped ambition, false desires and intermittent happiness.

Growing up in Atlanta, the main male figure in my life was my grandfather. For all of my life, I had known him to be blind. So I would attend meetings with him, luncheons and dinners, and just be around to help him alongside my aunt. As I grew in age and maturity, I began noticing how my grandfather interacted with people, and even more so, how they interacted with him. He had a calming demeanor. Initially, I assumed that because he was blind that he was just a calm person. But I later realized his demeanor was calming because he was calm.

People always seemed to be happy to see him and shake his hand. Maybe they were just being kind, but I could see that most of them genuinely cared about him, and were happy to be around him. People would come by the house (his and my grandmother's house) and sit in the dining room to talk about family, the community, or even business. And people always seemed to have this sort of reverence towards him; similar to my favorite movie character, *The Godfather*. But underneath all of his exterior, I sensed a heart that was filled with service. He always spoke about being kind to my parents, and to people period. He donated his money and attended every community event that he could gather the strength to participate in. And he exuded the spirit of what is commonly regarded as servant leadership.

My grandfather was a postman much of his life and went on to serve in the Georgia General Assembly when President Carter was governor. I remember meeting

President Carter in the mid-1980s. He was speaking in Atlanta and my grandfather had tickets to the event. Once President Carter was done speaking my grandfather asked me to take him outside to the side door where the President would exit so he could speak with him.

I had no clue that my grandfather knew the former President. And I was also a little hesitant to take him to speak to this man he said he knew. But I did as I was told and off we went to the side door. As expected, President Carter finally made his way over to the exit we were at (I still don't know how he knew what exit he would go to). But before I could tell my grandfather that the President was walking towards us, President Carter exclaimed in a welcoming voice, "Clarence, great seeing you!" And the rest was history. They talked and my grandfather introduced me and low and behold, he knew President Carter really well. But that was my granddad. I learned that day of just how well he did know the President. My grandfather supported him during his presidential campaign. Later on, in life, I would find actual inauguration invitations addressed to my grandfather...the actual invitations!

People loved him and over time I understood why. He was as kind as they come. He would always tell me, "Sparky, I want you to be kind to people." I heard him say it, but I didn't fully understand those words and what they would mean to me later on in life. He showed me how to serve others; how to be kind, and generous, and care for others unconditionally. His life was a selfless one. Whether or not his blindness was a contributing factor is for others to speculate, but I knew a man who exhibited kindness to others that I strive to live up to daily.   He was my first authentic example of joy.

After having job after job, making money, losing money, making more money, and losing more money, I realized that money was not my issue; joy was my issue. I looked back at my time with my grandfather and suffered in silence because I didn't listen more and spend more time with him. But I knew that I had to get over that and move on. I knew the best way to honor him was to do what he always shared with me - *be kind*.

So I decided to seek that path; a path of genuine kindness, a path of selflessness, a path of joy.   That journey led me to know one thing - all I wanted to do in my life was to serve others. It was inside of me. It was my gift that I knew was there with me always. I saw my gift manifest itself in so many places in my life, but I had not cultivated or nourished it. It's what I was most grateful for and I knew that my purpose in life would always be in service to others. There it was, right where I stood.   Gratitude to serve, and purpose to serve others.   My life was in fact *joy*.   My grandfather lived a life of joy every single day he drew breathe. Blind, with a cane, he lived better than most seeing and walking human beings. And he did it because he lived a purpose-driven life.   If you think about it, we are all here to serve. Aside from what we believe matters in life, service is the gift of a life well-lived.

Joy is like being in a zone, you just can't miss. When you have joy in your life, even when things are bumpy, everything around you feels like you are sailing with a breeze at your back. And once you get in that zone it's a life you can hardly explain to others, because it frees you from so many constraints and burdens that you have been allowing to exist in your heart and head. If you are having a hard time determining whether or not you have joy in your life, there is a distinct possibility that you may not. And that's ok, but it's time that you begin to determine if you want to just walk through your life, or do you want to enjoy your life.

Once I landed my first paying client I became a believer that I could do what I was passionate about in life. It didn't matter the amount of money because if I stepped into greatness only God knew what financial benefits would come my way. My job was to focus on my purpose, my God-given gift, and work with intention. This is where joy takes over and excuses are crushed.

Eventually, opportunities began to become present as if God was just waiting for me to get serious about the business of serving others. A call from a friend to come speak at their place of work, a referral from a non-fee event I facilitated a year earlier, and even a contract that came out of an informal lunch meeting. These blessings were happening because I shifted into joy. And joy allows me to reset my entire way of listening, seeing and feeling, and receiving the gifts that life has to offer.

I began to operate as a servant leader, separating the qualitative from the quantitative. It no longer mattered to me how much I could make on a contract. What mattered was that the client was willing to take the journey with me; that was qualitative. And whatever their budget was we would make it work - that was quantitative.

My family life situation was continually leveling out. As a husband, I was still a work in progress, but at least it was in progress. The challenge of dealing with both intra-personal struggles and inter-personal struggles began to make sense. Living a joyous life created another reality for me, for our family. Was it perfect? No, but it began to have a light shine inside me, and that's what joy brings. Joy can exist in the darkest of times because you are not relying on fleeting emotions.

After 2018 I was feeling more like life was making sense. Yeah, it took a while. I remember someone asking me how long did it take to get to where I was able to see clearly. I responded by simply saying, "I'm still working on it, I'll get back to you in twenty more years." A little of me was being silly, but the truth is that God's plan for our lives is an infinite one. And though you may come to a place that has you seeing clearer, making better choices, and living a more purpose-driven life, we still are growing.

My purpose in the world is to *"inspire people to love more abundantly, passionately, and unconditionally, in the service and care of others."* To me, this purpose statement will have me expanding and growing until the day I tilt over and leave this world. It's audacious on purpose. And it challenges me every minute of my life.

Earlier in the book, I spoke about a time in college when I had a moment with God in a church service. I cried out to God to help me and to tell me what He wanted from me on earth. I was searching, asking that famed old question about purpose. God's specific plan for me (as if I really know) has had me in some tough times. I felt broken, but I was whole; I believed I couldn't go on, but I did. I couldn't see clearly, but

He guided me and spoke in my heart wisdom and patience. Whether you are a believer in God, or just a spiritual person, or even a non-believer - I know in every breathe I take that if we can commit to joy - reflecting on the blessed experiences in our lives, we can do the heart work that it takes to wake up each day with gratitude, purpose, and love.

I joy

Expression #9: I recall being asked what is the difference between being happy and being joyous. It's fairly simple to explain; happiness is fleeting. One can be happy in a moment that can be immediately followed by sadness; they both are emotional states that will not exist simultaneously. On the other hand, joy can live in all states of emotion. Joy can be present during happiness and sadness because joy is a state of heart and mind. Joy is not solely an emotion, it's a conscious commitment to gratitude and living with purpose.

When you are filled with gratitude and led with selfless purpose, you can rest assure that you are living a life of joy. You may have read, "Joy comes in the morning" (*Psalm 30:5*). What does this mean? Does it mean no matter what happens in life joy will be present in the morning? This verse poses an interesting question: are we able to experience joy, even in the midst of a tremendous storm?

The Bible verse speaks of the weeping that comes before joy, and we experience weeping moments in our lives that feels as if the world is ending. They are painful, hurtful, crushing moments that can render us immobile. But does this type of weeping mean joy can't be present? I used to wonder how people who had so little, could rejoice so much; and people who had so much could rejoice so little. To paraphrase Gary Vaynerchuk...*the fact is, there are two realities in this world - there is someone out there who has less than you, and has more joy than you; and there is someone out there that has more than you, and has less joy than you.*

Joy Exercise

Life can seem so complex while being so simple at the same time. We can choose to live with joy or exist without it. But whichever we choose, it is indeed a choice. This exercise serves one purpose: to allow you an opportunity to choose; joy or no joy.

Instructions: Answer the following ten questions. Once completed, write an overview of what you will choose in your life to live with joy.

Q1: How do you define joy?

Q2: What does joy look like in your life?

Q3: What to you is beautiful in life?

Q4: What is holding you back (if anything) from living a joyous life?

Q5: What is the first thing you would do to enjoy yourself if you could do anything?

Q5: Do you have a big dream? Something that you have always wanted to do, but never took the time to do it.

Q6: What is holding you back from going after your dreams? Why?

Q7: Are you fearful of pursuing your dreams? Are you fearful of living out your dreams?

Q8: What will it take for you to take the first step in fulfilling your dreams?

Q9: Are you ready to begin moving your life towards joy? If yes, complete Q10.

Q10: Write down the one dream you want to fulfill. Then write down how this dream will reveal the joy inside of you.

After completing this exercise and answering the questions, ask yourself this question: Do I want to find my joy, or reveal my joy? If you answered reveal my joy, then you are on your way. There is no finding joy; joy is within you. Your dreams, your passions, and all the goodness inside your spirit reflect your center of joy. Look into what "joy" means and how it relates to your life. I firmly believe that you already have a place inside of you that is waiting to express your inner-joy (Remember: think gratitude, purpose, love)

NOTES:

_____

_____

_____

_____

_____

_____

_____

_____

_____

_____

_____

_____

_____

_____

_____

_____

_____

_____

_____

_____

_____

HEART WORK

Now that you have completed reading and working through the first nine chapters, I pray that my story and the principles (expressions) that were shared have in some way inspired you to continue on your heart work journey. The first nine chapters are focused on an intrapersonal experience, with plenty of introspection and personal self-reflection.

The next part of this book is focused on connecting your intrapersonal development with your interpersonal development. The following learning and development exercises will challenge you to have more thoughtful reflections and inquiry with yourself and your team.

I have only piece of advice; take your time and don't rush through the exercises while having these necessary learning experiences and conversations. Cheers to your heart work!

I Heart Work

Heart Work is a series of leadership development exercises based on research and leader practitioner experiences. These forums have been facilitated to hundreds of leaders from a variety of professional sectors and industries. Before beginning the *Heart Work Expression Forums*, here is an overview and a few facilitator guidelines that we recommend:

1) The **Discussion Review** provides participants with an overview of the topic and five discussion questions *(approx. time with group: 20 min). The responses provided are to help guide your discussion, and are not a representation of "the only answer."*

2) The **Expression Overview** provides participants with a 1) more in-depth background on the topic *(approx. time with group: 20 min),* 2) a Group Exercise *(approx. time with group: 30 min),* and 3) Practical Application review questions/strategies *(approx. time with group: 15 min).* These timeline guidelines apply to the recommended level of up to twenty (20) participants.
   - *These time parameters are flexible and should only be used as guides. Allow for your discussions to evolve naturally, while still maintaining structure as to not detour too much off of the central topic.*
   - *But first, please take time to review the learning questionnaire. It will be helpful in crafting the appropriate group discussions that will relate best with your team.*

Learning & Development

For leaders/teams that want to understand the culture, context, application, and measurement strategies of learning organizations.

Learning Questionnaire

Thank you for taking the first step towards a transformational experience for you and your organization. This learning questionnaire was created to gain clearer insight into critical factors of organizational learning. At Leadership Matters Group we use this questionnaire in a variety of formats. And our primary mission is to ensure that our client-partners are prepared, knowledgeable, and able to receive an optimal learning experience that adds value to their organization.

Studies have shown that approximately 70% of in-person learning does not translate into positive business outcomes. Factors that are typically not considered are culture, context, application, and measurement strategies.

We address these factors by asking meaningful and introspective questions. Because you should aim to be as knowledgable as you can be before supporting your leaders during formal leadership development experiences. These questions are not an exhaustive list, but we can assure you that your responses will provide clarity to these critical areas of your organization.

In 2014, McKinsey and Company published an article examining the four ways in which companies could gain more from leadership development engagements (Gurdjian, et al, 2014). The following learning questionnaire covers (for your use) the four areas that will enable you to achieve just what McKinsey & Co. posit are the necessary building blocks of effective learning.

Learning Questionnaire

Discussion: Before beginning "Heart Work," please discuss the following factors in learning & development. What questions are you asking your leaders before creating learning experiences for them? If you are asking these questions, awesome! But, if you are not, take some time to review and discuss them in small groups to gain some insight into how your team responds.

Culture is...
The existence of shared values and beliefs.

1) *Why do you like working here? What motivates you to come to work every day?*

2) *How important is leadership development perceived by teammates?*

3) *How does the company address/celebrate failure? And success?*

4) *Is there collaboration within teams and across different ones?*

5) *How does the company address personal well-being (the total health of team members)?*

Context is...

How you define your current circumstances.

1) What have been growth points for the organization?

2) How would you rate the team's capacity to perform?

3) How are you developing your strongest leaders?

4) If you did nothing at all for leaders, what would happen?

5) Are you where you thought the organization would be?

Application is...

The transfer of learning concepts to implementation.

1) If you could only work on one project for a year, what would it be and why?

2) Are leaders held accountable to apply learning to real issues on the job?

3) What are leader expectations regarding implementing new learning?

4) Who is facilitating a specific plan for the back-at-work application of learning?

5) What follow-up is present for leaders to translate learning into action?

The measure is...

How you assess the quality and impact of learning.

1) How would you explain the process in which you measure success?

2) What team members are involved in developing success measures?

3) How do you measure knowledge (learning)?

4) How do you know learning has taken place after development exercises?

5) Does your team adapt well while learning new information?

PART I

HEART

For leaders/teams that seek to discover how the heart guides one's path in leadership and life.

I heart intelligence

DISCUSSION REVIEW

Heart Intelligence is defined as your awareness and understanding of the connections between your heart, mind, and emotions. It is the starting point of your ability to be present and conscious in all of your being. Huh? LOL! I know, it's not as complex as it may sound. *Heart Intelligence*, though critically debated, is a very real thing if you believe that our heart has an intuitive guidance that helps us balance our emotions. Simply put, the heart and mind are always guiding our emotional state. And because of this, our ability to tap into our heart's intelligence is even more important in our evolving world. As leaders contemplate how to prepare to lead in an ever-changing workforce, how they lead from the heart - its intelligence, will certainly be the greatest asset they will have to inspire teams to strive for greatness.

Q1: What do we know about heart intelligence? *The heart and brain are constantly communicating with each other, which allows for our intuitive senses to be activated so that we quickly can feel and sense what's happening with us and around us.*

Q2: Why does heart intelligence matter? *When we can listen more deeply to our hearts, we can experience more peace, better health, and greater joy in our lives.*

Q3: What are the obstacles to attaining heart intelligence? *Dealing with high levels of stress, anxiety, anger, and an inability to relax are critical challenges.*

Q4:   What are the benefits of activating your heart intelligence?   *Develop more loving, harmonious relationships; having the ability to create greater life alignment and improve your mental and emotional capacity regardless of your circumstances.*

Q5:   What are the strategies we can use to increase our heart intelligence?   *Practice heart-centered breathing (5 seconds in, 5 seconds out).   Practice daily (preferably morning) gratitude affirmations.   Take time to practice self-reflection, quietly, feeling all of what you are experiencing and being present in your state of being (even if it is challenging).*

HEART INTELLIGENCE

Expression #10 (Overview)

Heart Intelligence is not the most discussed topic in academia or workplace environments. So why should we investigate and/or utilize its principles? For one, all human beings have hearts and minds that work together in ways that can transform the physiology and psychology of our existence. The connectedness and coherent alignment of our heart, mind, and emotions are how early theorists define heart intelligence. But you don't have to theorize about the relationship between your heart, mind, and emotions. Just look at the research on the power of the heart and how the heart feels when you are in emotional or mental pain - *the relationship between depression and heart disease is a two-way street...not only does depression appear to promote heart disease, but it can also result from a heart attack (Harvard Medical School, 2020).*

Group Exercise: *My Story is my Super-Power*

Our stories are not meant to shame us, but to guide us from the heart. This discussion and exercise requires you to process your story in three steps: acknowledgment, acceptance, and alignment.

Quick Discussion: Discuss and examine how stories are an instrumental tool (inspirational and informational) to self-discovery and interpersonal connection.

This exercise is designed to challenge your current thinking and doing as it relates to using your story for a greater good. A "lifestream" is an opportunity for you to reflect and demonstrate through art and storytelling your life's experiences; those experiences that make you, you. It is a form of storytelling that allows you to capture how you see your life and share those elements of your life that are important to you *(Ex.: A lifestream can include a diagram of words, art, or a combination of both that depicts your life story in the manner you wish to share).*

Instructions: The participant will first draw out their lifestream on paper (any type of paper or drawing paper) provided by the facilitator. Once completed, the leader will respond to the following statements: (Using your lifestream as a guide)

1.Write down some key life obstacles and successes on a piece of paper. (Acknowledgement)

2. Take your thoughts and write a summary story of what your lifestream says about you. (Acceptance)

3. Now, summarize how your story aligns with your life, your future. (Alignment)

Practical Application: Now, in a small group, listen and share with your group. Answer the following questions, and discuss how you can incorporate stories into your organizational culture.

1) How does it feel to share your story?

2) How does it feel to hear someone else's story?

3) What takeaways are present to you in this exercise?

4) Where do you see stories being an asset in your role as a leader?

5) How would you incorporate "telling stories" in your work environment?

HEART-CENTERED LEADERSHIP

Heart-centered leadership can exist in all human beings; it encompasses leading with love, extending compassion, and providing others what they need and want through service. This happens when both leader and follower feel safe to trust, be vulnerable, and show courage in the face of the unknown. Have you ever had an experience that was so moving that you felt it in your heart?

Quick Exercise: Write down what comes to mind when you think about heart-centered leadership.

Discuss and examine how your personal experience within your organization reflects a healthy heart culture or not. Based on the heart intelligence and heart-centered leadership overviews, where do you see comparisons (or not) to your organization?

Group Exercise: *Heart Care*

This exercise is designed to challenge your current thinking and doing as it relates to your heart intelligence. The three areas of focus to gain greater heart intelligence and heart-centered leadership are forgiveness, gratitude, self-care. Each participant will answer a set of questions first and then write their responses down. Then, the group will report out in the small group. Finally, small groups will report out to the entire group.

The statements/questions are as follows:

1) Rate your ability to forgive, on a scale of 1 - 5 (1, not at all forgiving; 5, very forgiving)

2) Rate how much you practice gratitude, on a scale of 1 - 5 (1, not at all; 5, very often)

3) How much do you practice quiet time, meditation, or slow breathing, on a scale of 1 - 5? (1, not at all; 5, very often)

Practical Application: Ask yourself how your organization can highlight the importance of heart care, and implement useful strategies that will engage your team to develop behaviors that will improve their heart intelligence.

1) What can we do as a team to bring attention to heart care/ heart-centered leadership?

2) How can we incorporate heart care activities in our work environment?

3) How can we be accountable to each other as heart-centered leaders?

4) What stakeholders need to be in the conversation when we discuss heart-centered leadership?

5) How close/far are we to achieving a more heart-centered culture?

PART II

MIND
For leaders/teams that seek to discover how the mind equips us to think broader, clearer, and with intention.

I design thinking

DISCUSSION REVIEW

Design thinking is a human-centered approach using design methods for human needs that add value. The future of heart-centered leadership and organizational learning will undoubtedly be influenced by the evolution of design thinking. What leaders learn, how they apply learning, and how organizations are impacted through learning is and will be directly connected to leaders who develop design thinking as a leadership attribute.

Q1: What do we know about design thinking? *Design thinking is not a new phenomenon; it has been historically associated with product design and tactical thought, and now it is also associated with the creation of societal solutions.*

Q2: Why does design thinking matter? *Design thinking challenges us to think about who we are serving before we think about how we serve them. The future of how organizations not only learn but how they serve their internal and external stakeholders directly correlates to how leaders think - design think more specifically.*

Q3: What are the obstacles to becoming a design thinker? *Having limiting beliefs, not having a vision, and being disconnected from people and their existence or realities.*

Q4: What are the benefits of becoming a design thinker? *Create products, cultures, and experiences that people want and need. Serve in a deeper, more meaningful way by first seeking to understand the experiences of others.*

Q5:   What are the strategies we can use to implement design thinking traits? *Begin to integrate the key attributes of a design thinker into all that you do...policies, processes, and culture must be rooted in design thinking.*

DESIGN THINKING: *Expression #11 (Overview)*

Tim Brown (2008) defines design thinking as a *"discipline that uses the designer's sensibility and methods to match people's needs with what is technologically feasible and what a viable business strategy can convert into customer value and market opportunity."* Simply put, in design thinking, one creates with the end (customer or societal issue) in mind.

Group Exercise: *THINK Big*

This group exercise requires each small group to *THINK Big*...putting your creative ideas and passions to work, you are charged to come up with an audacious idea using the *personality attributes of a design thinker.* This idea should be something that you can implement in your workplace for the benefit of your team or your company *(Think about a process, system, or project that can help improve your organization).*

Personality Attributes of a Design Thinker (Brown, 2008)

1) *Empathy - Understanding and sharing the feelings/ existence of others*

2) *Integrative Thinking - Solving complex problems with a multi-cooperative scale of thought*

3) *Optimism - Hope and positive outlook*

4) *Experimentalism - Truth through experimenting/trying*

5) *Collaboration - Working with others to achieve something*

Instructions: *During this exercise, and after developing your "big idea," you will share with your group the following:*

1) What is your "big idea"?

2) Specific attributes you use to engage with your team to develop your idea

3) Some successes and/or opportunities you can improve on during your development process

4) What you would change if anything in your approach (use intensive self-reflection and critical analysis of your mindset and behavior)

Practical Application: Now, as you return to your teams/organizations, Brown (2008) suggests that you "...teach people how to land before they jump."

Design Thinking happens through the process of Inspiration, Ideation, Implementation.

1) How will we introduce (talk about with team members) design thinking to stakeholders?

2) How will we integrate design thinking in our culture (ie. personal discovery, practical application, team development)?

3) How do we operationalize design thinking?

4) How will we hold ourselves accountable?

5) How will we evaluate and measure success/failure?

GROWTH MINDSET

Having a *Growth Mindset* is central to leaders exhibiting foresight, hope, and will. Leaders often face challenging obstacles, and they sometimes must make decisions that place them in tenuous positions. Having a fixed or growth mindset undoubtedly affects leaders ability to lead effectively. Limiting beliefs will derail teams even with the best talent and intentions. The question for leaders who seek to empower culture, is *"how does one inspire others to believe in the I'm-possible growth mindset?"*

Group Exercise: *The I'm-possible Growth Mindset*

I think we all can remember the slogan, "A mind is a terrible thing to waste." And indeed, our mindset is one of the most important tools that we have in our toolbox. If we can activate the inner-most powerful components of our mind, there is nothing we can't achieve. This group exercise challenges you to access your extreme ability by not considering failure, but embracing the growth and learning that takes place when we push ourselves to use our growth mindset that everything is possible.

Instructions: Each group is charged to create the tallest tower they can build, using only post-it notes (1 stack), straws (20), and paper clips (40). There are two rules - participants must use all of the materials provided to them and nothing can be attached to the ceiling. Each group has a total of 5 minutes to discuss strategy and 10 minutes to build their tower. (This exercise can also be performed virtually)

After completing the tower, each group must report out on the following questions:

1) What was the group strategy on building the tower?

2) *Did the group collectively believe a standing tower could be built?*

3) *What talents did each member contribute to the process?*

4) *What did each member learn during the process?*

5) *What would you do differently, if anything?*

Practical Application: When you think of your organizational culture, do you think of it being a growth culture? Does your organization develop ideas from a growth mindset? Why or why not? Ask yourself these questions:

1) *How can we incorporate growth mindset principles into our daily workplace experiences?*

2) *What would happen if we began to think through a growth lens?*

3) *What could our organization accomplish if we empowered leaders to believe in the I'm-possible?*

4) *Where should we begin (brainstorming meetings, innovation thought hubs, project leader selection)?*

5) *What should be our first "big idea" for our organization?*

PART III

WELLNESS

For leaders/teams that seek to learn how wellness empowers them to be healthy, focused, and productive.

I psychological wellness

DISCUSSION REVIEW

Psychological wellness is defined by Cowen (1994) as "having effective broad facets associated with psychological markers, having a sense of belonging and purpose, control over one's fate and satisfaction with one's existence and oneself." Psychological wellness (purpose) is the life-changing, transformational part of life that splashes water on your face in the morning, kicks you in the rear, and powers you up to make your mark in a world that awaits your gift.

Q1: What do we know about psychological wellness? *Belonging...Purpose...are both within every living creature. And our psychological wellness is influenced by a choice that we make to either wait for someone to affirm for us our rightful existence or affirm for ourselves our self-worth and value.*

Q2: What are the obstacles to attaining psychological wellness? *Lack of or low emotional intelligence; absence of self-worth and a fear of facing personal trials and obstacles.*

Q3: Why does psychological wellness matter? *It creates and embodies meaningful social connectivity, and personal joy and purpose. Without it, we struggle to connect with our sense of belonging and connection to the broader world.*

Q4: What are the benefits of having psychological wellness? *Humans exhibit more vulnerability and courage, with greater opportunities for increased learning, innovation, and performance.*

Q5: What are the steps/strategies we need to adopt to evolve our state of being psychologically well? *Start where you are - Assess, Evaluate, Affirm, Collaborate, Design (Integrate these facets associated with optimal psychological wellness (Ryff, 1995)). If we can follow these steps, we can uncover just how to reveal our greatest sense of value and psychological wellness.*

PSYCHOLOGICAL WELLNESS: *Expression #12 (Overview)*

Psychological wellness defines everything that we care about and value in our lives; it's the very idea that we have purpose and direction. Researchers Ryan and Deci (2000) have identified six components of psychological wellness: *1) autonomy, 2) competence, 3) healthy relationships, 4) self-acceptance, 5) personal growth, and 6) purpose in life.* Interestingly enough, one could presume that humans struggle with purpose the most. Do you know what your purpose is in life? Are you thinking about purpose? Do you know where to begin? Sometimes these questions can make us feel lost, not prepared, or even just weary. But your purpose shouldn't frighten you, it should invigorate you. Purpose evolves; purpose can shift. Uncovering it should be a wondrous journey, filled with reflection, discovery, aha moments, and inspiration. There is no denying that purpose is powerful.

Group Exercise: *A Balancing Act*

Achieving psychological wellness can take a tremendous amount of time and effort to process and figure out the many questions you have about yourself, and life as a whole. A key piece to this process is understanding the balance and direction of your life.

Instructions: During this exercise, you are being asked to rank on a scale from 1 - 5 (1, not well; 5, extremely well) how you see yourself achieving balance in five areas of your life:

1) Spending quality time with family and/or friends

2) Reading books, articles, or anything educational or inspirational

3) Writing in a journal or notes about your personal and/or professional life

4) Doing something fun/exciting daily or weekly

Am I falling short, meeting, or exceeding balance in my life? Why or why not?

Practical Application: Within this type of *psychological wellness* culture, we check in more and we give more of ourselves because we relate an interpersonal connection with our deep-rooted commitment to each other.

Answer the following questions for your organization:

1) Within your team, how are you creating this type of culture?

2) How are you connecting to teammates to increase their sense of belonging?

3) What is working? What is falling short? How will you move forward?

I physical wellness

DISCUSSION REVIEW

Physical wellness encourages the balance of physical activity, nutrition, and mental well-being to keep your body in top condition (shcs.ucdavis.edu). No matter if you are caring for your mental, emotional, or physical wellness, the human body requires that you care for all of you not just pieces of you. Through what and how you eat, how you manage your emotions, and how you treat your body, physical wellness is influenced and affected by all that you do and don't do.

Q1: What do we know about physical wellness? *Physical wellness is attributed to healthier living, greater emotional capacity, and living a longer life. All of who we are can be associated with how much we pay attention and invest in our physical wellness.*

Q2: What are the obstacles to attaining physical wellness (personally, professionally, etc.)? *Fear of trying and lack of time; a lack of understanding of how to take care of our bodies, minds, and emotions, and minimal support systems/surroundings that help to enrich our spirits and resources.*

Q3: Why does it matter? *Increases energy level for greater productivity and reduces the risk of disease. Increases cognitive ability and improves self-confidence and self-image (www.heart.org).*

Q4: What are the benefits of physical wellness? *Achieve greater performance and increased leadership competencies; learning increases and ultimately supports greater levels of* *creativity. Exercise affects the brain by increasing the heart rate and pumping more oxygen to the brain (www.heart.org).*

Q5:   What are the steps/strategies we need to adopt to achieve physical wellness?   *Start small, make plans (meals, workout regiment, check-ups); channel willpower at its highest peak (morning or afternoon) and make a list of self-care activities that can be performed at home and work.*

PHYSICAL WELLNESS: *Expression #13 (Overview)*

The way we treat our bodies is telling; most people in the industrialized world have heard of or know something about physical wellness.   For decades, television shows, entertainers, and health gurus have demonstrated how physical wellness influences the entirety of our lives. One can posit that a fit leader is likely to be a more effective leader. Physical wellness creates more energy for greater productivity, more confidence for inspired creativity, and more focus that drives direction.   The Mayo Clinic sites that *exercise even reduces symptoms associated with feelings of anxiety and depression.* But physical wellness doesn't stop at exercising; the food we eat affects our bodies just as much as the stressors and negative feelings we allow.

Group Exercise: *Body Building*

No, don't be scared...I am not at all expecting you to become a bodybuilder in the traditional sense of the term.   But, I am specifically referencing the process of building up your physical body, so that you are physically well. This exercise is designed for you to examine your overall physical wellness. The US Department of Health & Human Services states that adults should aim for 150 minutes of moderate aerobic exercise and two strength-training sessions per week.   And according to an article in *Psychology Today*, physical activity is the best way to improve cognitive function (Duncan, 2014). And research has shown that balanced diets, sleep, and self-care all contribute to a person's over-all physical wellness.

Instructions: Take one sheet of paper and write down the following four activities in four evenly spaced boxes.

1) 20 minutes of moderate aerobic daily exercise (ref: US Dept. HHS)

2) *A daily balanced diet and healthy outcomes (ref: The Science Behind Healthy Eating Outcomes)*

3) *Minimum of seven (7) hours of sleep within a 24-hr period (ref: The National Sleep Foundation)*

4) *Personal reflection time (this could include spiritual reflection, quiet time, or meditation) (ref: NIH.org)*

Next, tear/cut the boxes out into four pieces and select the boxes that you consistently complete on a daily basis. The boxes that you are unable to select, you will place into the middle of your group table. Discuss with your group why you have not been able to complete these activities. Then share how you will design your future physical wellness by creating a *body building* plan.

Practical Application: Now, how will you address physical wellness with your team?   Leading can be tough and challenging on your mental state of mind, and equally draining on your physical wellness.   While we normally associate physical health with physical appearance, our physical wellbeing affects our entire body, inside and out.

1) *How does your leadership team show your commitment to everyone's physical wellness?*

2) *How is your team encouraging physical wellness within your organization?*

3) *What resources are available, that are easy to access and/ or affordable?*

4) *Through what means are leaders learning about the physical wellness of team members (surveys, physical wellness events, etc.)?*

I social wellness

DISCUSSION REVIEW

Social Wellness involves developing healthy relationships with those you interact with and come into contact with during your life. Having friends isn't the qualifying attribute of being socially well. But having people in your life that you trust, feel comfortable being around, and can turn to in good and bad times are key qualities in socially well people.

Q1: What do we know about social wellness? *Being honest and supportive strengthens relationships and devoting time to developing relationships is valuable; and healthy relationships can improve overall health.*

Q2: What are the obstacles to attaining social wellness? *Personal trauma and/or negative personal experiences and personal attitude towards developing relationships. An absence of self-awareness of unhealthy behaviors.*

Q3: What are the habits most needed to attain social wellness? *Willingness to be open to new behaviors. Active listening and intentionally engaging with others are key to building authentic connections.*

Q4: Why does it matter? *Relationships are inextricably connected to personal health; human connectivity is a foundational element for emotional health and healthier relationships can be an indicator of personal growth. Social wellness affects our overall attitude about life and those in our lives.*

Q5: What are the steps/strategies we need to adopt for social wellness? *Four steps to social wellness: 1) Practice self-care 2) Start to learn "you" 3) Nurture new friendships and rekindle old friendships 4) Don't criticize, judge, or blame.*

SOCIAL WELLNESS: *Expression #14 (Overview)*

As I write this paragraph, our world is currently in a place of physical disconnection *(the 2020 COVID-19 Pandemic)*, that has led us to feel socially disconnected, even with the most robust social media platforms ever to have existed. I can say with certainty, as a country and world, we are not feeling socially well. So, as we journey into a disconnected unknown state, the one question that we should be asking is, "How *socially well* were we before the 2020 COVID-19 pandemic began?"

Being socially well is more than just having friends or being popular on social media. Social wellness is truly about having a sense of belonging in society; being connected to others in a manner that brings you joy and peace. Social wellness is essential to our existence...*developing and maintaining social networks, creating boundaries that encourage trust and communication and having a support network of friends & family to connect and enjoy life with (University of New Hampshire, 2020).*

Group Exercise: *Social Science*

Researchers suggest that a person's social connection to others is a key indicator of the wellness of a person's mental and emotional state. In this exercise, you are being asked to take part in a social science experiment. This exercise will challenge you to reach out to friends/family, not to just be social but to get re-connected. Remember, life is not defined by the number of people we are connected to, its defined by the quality of our connections with the people in our lives.

Instructions: Open up your phone or address book. Who are the five people in your contacts that you haven't spoken with in over 30 days (90 days max)? Well, it's time to reach out and reconnect with them. First, write down their names and either shoot them a text or give them a brief call (whichever is best for your time parameters). Next, write down how the communication unfolded. What did it feel like to re-connect? How did they respond? Does this exercise make you want to reach out to others that you haven't connected with lately?

Practical Application: Social wellness is often disguised in company culture activities that suggest if team members hang out together once a quarter after work, or have ping-pong tables in the lunch-room, they will feel more like a team - more connected. But organizational cultures that authentically promote and intentionally invest in social wellness ask the following questions:

1) How do our team members address their social wellness?

2) What do we do as an organization to encourage social wellness behaviors in the workplace?

3) How does social wellness make meaningful contributions to our workplace culture?

4) How can we make social wellness a priority in our organization?

5) Who in our organization should spearhead and contribute to the planning of social wellness initiatives?

I emotional wellness

DISCUSSION REVIEW

Emotional wellness is the awareness, understanding, and acceptance of our feelings, and our ability to manage effectively through challenges and change. We all experience the circular nature of life. And how we respond is arguably more important than what it is we are responding to. Our emotional wellness is one of the aspects of life that organizational leaders seldom address, but undoubtedly is one of the most important. How we recognize, manage, and address our emotions, and the emotions of others is critical to how we show up in life's most complex circumstances.

Q1: What do we know about emotional wellness? *Our emotions are triggered by different experiences, and our ability to manage our emotions is paramount to responding to stress, exhibiting a positive attitude, and having a strong mindset.*

Q2: What are the obstacles to attaining emotional wellness? *Overloaded professional workloads, the inability for employees to take needed vacations, and self-care not being a professional/personal priority contribute to decreased emotional wellness.*

Q3: What is the path to attain emotional wellness? *Have a positive outlook on life, dealing with challenges when they happen, giving yourself grace in moments of difficulty, and celebrating life every chance you have.*

Q4: Why does emotional wellness matter? *People are driven in part by emotions, and emotional wellness has been scientifically correlated to happiness and self-worth.*

Psychological and physical health are influenced by emotions, in turn influencing the environment in which we exist.

Q5: **What are the steps/strategies we need to adopt to evolve our state of being emotionally well?** *Kolakowski (2013) states that to experience greater emotional wellness we must lead a more purposeful life, adopt a value-centric mindset, and exhibit patience while treating others well.*

EMOTIONAL WELLNESS - *Expression #15 (Overview)*

For the past three decades, emotional intelligence has been front and center of everything related to leadership and personal development. Emotional wellness is equally important and critical to the overall emotional stability of leaders, and wellness is accomplished by reaching a high level of emotional intelligence. Human-beings are often cautious about admitting how emotional we can become. But, in fact, we are emotional; we feel immensely, and we react on a spectrum of emotions, rational and otherwise. Emotional wellness is about seeking self-care and having an inner strength to confront the positives and negatives in life. The National Institute of Health (NIH) defines the benefits of emotional wellness as having resilience, reduced stress levels, and mindfulness.

Group Exercise: *Laugh Out Loud*

Laughing is just simply refreshing; even for the most introverted person, one would be hard-pressed to find someone who doesn't enjoy a good laugh. There have been several studies that demonstrate how laughter influences better health outcomes in human beings. A study from the University of Maryland Medical System (umms.org) found that a sense of humor can even protect against heart disease (Shah, 2014). So if laughter can protect you from such a devastating disease, think of all the possibilities if we decided to laugh more often and out loud.

Instructions: This exercise insists you have some fun; to remind yourself just how good it feels to laugh, smile, and release all the messy stuff that we deal with every day. On a piece of paper, each participant should write down three downright hilarious experiences. (Be mindful, choose experiences that would not offend your teammates).

Next, share out in your small group by telling your stories, and don't forget to laugh out loud while you share. They may not be funny to the group, but I promise you, if you allow yourself to relive those moments, you will laugh regardless. Afterwards, in your larger group, discuss how telling those funny stories made you feel; how did your teammates respond? How would it make you feel if you could laugh out loud daily?

Practical Application: Now, think about the time you dedicate to laughing out loud, enjoying small yet meaningful moments with yourself and your team. Ask yourself:

1) *How would your teams feel if they were able to experience more laughter?*

2) *What could come from your team experiencing a more exciting culture?*

3) *After thinking about these questions, discuss with your leaders how your team can introduce creative and exciting ways to engage your team with laughter, more fun, and greater emotional wellness.*

Part IV

LEADership
Listen - Engage - Adapt - Deliver
For leaders/teams that seek to inspire, influence, and serve.

I listen

DISCUSSION REVIEW

Listening is the cornerstone of any meaningful and successful relationship. As listeners, we can be short-sighted, overly eager, and impatient, while wanting to just say our peace and move on. But I ask that you think about why we don't listen to understand, but more often choose to listen to respond. I challenge you to think about what it takes to be an authentic listener, vulnerable in your state of listening, and brave in your approach. Are you able to simply listen to others with a genuine desire to fully understand them?

Q1: What does it mean to listen effectively? *Being an active and mindful listener; genuinely interested in healthy exchanges and self and socially aware of the communicative circumstances.*

Q2: What challenges occur when seeking to listen? *Lack of trust between two people, a group, or organization; lack of forethought, fear of having difficult conversations, and exhibiting passive-aggressive attitudes.*

Q3: What interpersonal skills are necessary to listen to? *Presence - being available physically and mentally. Patience - exhibiting the ability to stay calm regardless of the circumstance. Empathy - having the ability to be understanding within the context of someone else's experience. Flexibility - being able to be open and/or have a willingness to compromise.*

Q4: Why does listening matter? *Awareness is essential in listening to achieve progress and growth. Leaders develop increased capacity by having meaningful exchanges and* *subsequently organizations are beneficiaries by being equipped to plan, organize, execute, and achieve greater impact.*

Q5: **What are the steps/strategies that leaders need to adopt in order to evolve their listening skills?** *Re-design business and human resource practices (standards, adaptations, expectations); intentionally integrate the key practices of effective communication into our culture and implement a leadership learning continuum on effective communication that is included in organizational training plans.*

LISTEN *to learn: Expression #16 (Overview)*

Listening is elevational. And, it can be transformational if you allow it. Listening should serve as a time when you are receiving, through all of your senses, without interjecting. This aspect of communication can be considered the purest form of demonstrating care. When relationships struggle with conflict, one could easily link the lack of listening to these challenges. In our role as leaders, a key component of our ability to influence, inspire, or even empower others directly correlates with listening. How are we listening? What are we listening for? And are we listening to everything we see/feel, and don't see/feel? If I were to tell you that your ability to effectively lead others is dependent on listening, what would you say? If I were to tell you that communication cultures are built on listening, how would you respond?

Group Exercise: *The Full Story*

360-degree listening is a practice in which a person isn't just listening to what the person is saying, but also how, and even what they aren't saying (Daimler, 2016). Our ability to recognize the verbal and non-verbal signals in communication through building trust is critical to developing successful relationships.

Instructions: This exercise challenges you to reflect and examine your 360-degree listening skills to understand the full story when communicating. First, each participant will take a piece of paper, draw a large circle on the paper, and divide the circle into four equal quadrants. Next, in each quadrant, write the following words: fear, anger, sadness, and anxiety. We will examine these words because they are often the emotions/states of mind that are hidden from us in communicating with others.

After completing this step, write down the verbal and non-verbal communication signals/behaviors associated with each of these emotions/states of mind. Once complete, answer the following questions for yourself:

1) What immediately stands out to you?

2) Have you missed some of these behaviors/signals before?

3) What will change for you, if anything, when listening to others?

4) What are some of your personal challenges when communicating?

5) How would you go about improving your communication with others?

Practical Application: What are some of the signals that your organization should be identifying while encouraging listening and effective communication?   What are the critical questions you should ask?   Take time to anonymously survey your teams on their thoughts and concerns related to organizational communication (use your 360-degree listening skills).   And then host open forums to brainstorm ideas, resources, and strategies that can help support an open, inclusive, and effective communication culture.

I engage

DISCUSSION REVIEW

Robert Greenleaf said, *"The first and most important choice a leader makes is the choice to serve."* Indeed, service to others is the ultimate reward of an engaging leader. Engaging leaders are looking deeper, seeking to develop connections based on genuine compassion and curiosity. They are passionately interested in learning *who you are, what you care about, and how they can be of service to you.* An engaged culture seeks to build trust, invest in people, and build open lines of communication throughout all levels of the organization.

Q1: What does it mean to be engaging? *To connect; develop a genuine relationship with others.*

Q2: What are the facts about engaged teams and leaders? *70% of American employees feel disengaged (Gallup, 2017). Disengaged employees affect culture and performance; 77% of managers want to engage (The Social Workplace, 2019). When leaders can authentically engage with teammates, organizational cultures become more welcoming and inclusive.*

Q3: What challenges occur when seeking to engage with people? *No clear personal desire; a lack of trust and/or psychological safety and no formal organizational engagement resources for teams to access.*

Q4: Why does it matter? *Engaging leaders achieve more impactful outcomes and engaged teams are happier and more productive. Engagement is fundamental for a healthy* team culture; people are an organization's greatest asset and people engagement should be a key priority.

Q5: What are the steps/strategies we need to adopt?
Measure engagement at all levels (all levels of leadership) and develop engaging leaders while instituting measures and rewards for meaningful engagement behaviors and impact.

ENGAGE *with compassion: Expression #17 (Overview)*

Engaging leaders exhibit heightened abilities to connect with others while eliciting feedback and ideas, building confidence in others, and creating a culture where teams feel valued and empowered. Research has found that *engaging with others* is a significant predictor of organizational performance, in contrast to leadership capabilities that did not predict performance (Alimo-Metcalfe, et al, 2008). Servant leadership is a key attribute of being an engaging leader. Empowering teams to grow and lead, inspiring teams to strive for personal and professional goals, and exhibiting patience through understanding self and others are the centerpieces of how leaders cultivate authentic connections.

Leadership Exercise: *Serve Your Team*

Leadership is service. This sentiment resonates deeply with me and hopefully, it does with you. When we think of engaging with others compassionately, in a meaningful way, it strikes me that we often forget that *serving* is the key when seeking to lead others.

Instructions: This exercise is designed to challenge your inner servant leader through creating an avenue to lead through service. Each small group will brainstorm on how they can channel a deeper connection with their teams by using engagement strategies to serve them better.

To begin, answer the following questions:

1) How do I personally define engagement?

2) Currently, how do I engage with my team?

3) What is working, what is falling short?

4) What are some ways I can improve engagement with my team?

5) How will I determine if the new strategies are working?

Next, after individually writing down your responses, the small group should discuss and create a master list of new strategies to better engage with and serve their teams. Remember, each team is unique and may require different approaches. Next, report out with the large group and discuss your ideas and thoughts.

Practical Application: Serving our teams can be a challenging task sometimes, even when we are armed with the best of intentions. What are you examining within your organization relating to the substantive behaviors of engagement with team members? Are you comfortable with your organization's engagement with your teams? Why or why not? How could you improve? Answering these questions is a start, but performing individual and group check-ins can provide you with meaningful feedback on how you can implement more impactful engagement strategies.

I adapt

DISCUSSION REVIEW

The ability and will to adapt *(especially in turbulent times)* is an invaluable attribute of every effective leader. The adaptable leader is one of the most sought after leaders in every organization. Why? Because organizations are complex institutions with nuances and dynamic components. And when the mess hits the fan, an adaptable leader shows up, leans in, and leads the team.

Q1: What does it mean to be adaptable? *Being adaptable is having the keen ability to adjust, re-direct, and be flexible while staying focused on a goal.*

Q2: What do we know about being adaptable? *Personal relationships increase your ability to respond to change and adapt. An open-minded attitude supports various perspectives and having core values allows for emotional stability through change. Deconstructing unwarranted stressful environments supports cognitive resilience and adjusting in turmoil.*

Q3: What challenges occur when seeking to be adaptable? *Lack of self-awareness and/or organizational cultural awareness; historical culture of "this is how we have always done it" and not cultivating and/or fostering a learning culture. An inability to be open to ambiguity.*

Q4: What are the three mindsets of an adaptable leader? *"Gamer - challenges us to apply courage and will power, and also optimism and creativity we have when applying fictional games to real-world problems; Beginner - rooted in openness, being childlike and curious. It's about asking "what if" and* *"why not" and not being dismissive; Growth - empowers you to take risks by freeing you from associating failure with your self-worth" (Dwane, 2016).*

Q5:   What are the steps/strategies that enable us to be adaptable? *Abandon the traditional mindset of rigid fixation and adopt an openness and willingness to practice adaptable behaviors in micro-wins. Over time incorporate behaviors that work well for you into your adaptation habits.*

ADAPT *in complexity - Expression #18 (Overview)*

Dynamic organizational cultures require that leaders are adaptable. More organizations are realizing that adaptable leaders will be the key to their future success. Consequently, being adaptable in complex environments has become an essential attribute of effective leadership.

Group Exercise: Calm in Complexity

Seriously, how calm are you during your most challenging times? How calm are you? Do you relax or do you get super frustrated in complexity? We all have our moments and not one of us is perfect. But, if you could resist stressing out during complexity, would you - could you? Let's try this exercise.

Instructions: This exercise is designed to help us replace anxiety and frustration with calm, rational, critical thinking and problem-solving so that we can channel our healthy thoughts and behaviors towards meaningful outcomes. First, read the scenario aloud to the entire group:

Case Scenario - A global pandemic has stricken the entire international community. Businesses are shutting down, schools are closing, cities and states are issuing shelter-in-home orders, and life as we know it has been relegated to virtual connectivity. Aside from essential workers and healthcare facilities, the entire world is essentially existing in an online world. Your Directive: As a leader within your organization, you are charged with laying off half of your 1,000 employees, and moving the remaining 500 employees to part-time employment. In addition to this administrative responsibility, you must also ensure that the 500 part-time employees are set-up with the necessary technology infrastructure and resources for them to do their jobs from home.

Next, answer the following questions for yourself and report out your thoughts in your small group, then have a discussion within your larger group on how you would go about responding to this type of scenario.

1) How do you feel?

2) How will you respond?

3) How will you communicate and engage with your teammates?

4) How will you adapt?

5) How will you support your teammates while they are forced to adapt to complexity?

6) Why or why not was this difficult for you?

7) Would you make the same decision again with more time to process? If not, what would be different?

8) How will you think differently about complexity?

9) How will you think differently about adaptability?

10)What one lesson have you learned from this exercise?

Practical Application: Ask yourself, "Would I be able to be calm in complexity and lead my team towards meaningful outcomes?" It's a question that doesn't have an easy answer. But one strategy to address complexity is to welcome it into your organization. Organizations, by design, are complex. And by acknowledging that complexity, you can create a real adaptive culture.

I deliver

DISCUSSION REVIEW

Steve Farber speaks of *showing proof* in his 2004 inspirational book, *The Radical Leap*. His primary theory is that extreme leaders must be willing to show proof, or as I like to say, *deliver* for their teams when the stakes matter the most. When leaders can deliver through investing their time, empowering their teams, and following through, everything is possible, and nothing can compare to the transformational leadership that happens when this behavior prevails.

Q1: What does it mean to *deliver*? *It means that you are a leader that understands your "why" - a leader who delivers and seeks to remove barriers so that teammates can succeed. S/he delivers for teammates by being honest, authentic, and of high moral character and integrity; and executes on commitments, even when the easier route may be to be passive, deflect, or just quit.*

Q2: What do we know about delivering impact? *To deliver for our teams, we must have a higher level of desire, commitment, and pure will to succeed for those we lead/serve.*

Q3: What challenges occur when seeking to deliver impact? *Results don't always happen the way we plan them or expect them to happen. Leaders must embody patience, resilience, and the ability to adapt to unforeseen circumstances. Additionally, delivering impact can be interrupted due to misinformation, impractical goals, and team dysfunction.*

Q4:   Why does it matter? *'Delivering' inspires and influences employees to do more than is required; adds personal value to the organization and its employees and creates a culture of healthy urgency.*

Q5:   What are the steps/strategies we need to adopt to deliver transformative impact? *Inspire with vision/motivate with guidance (strategy, tactics, resources); set audacious goals (make sure that the targets are difficult to achieve yet not impossible), and develop and coach the team.*

DELIVER *for your team - Expression #19 (Overview)*

Leaders must take care of themselves in order to best serve others. The best way to accomplish self-care is to invest in holistic health, be a lifelong learner, and commit to relaxing your mind and body. Delivering for your team means that you must also care for them, and love them. To *deliver* for your team, you must be in a position to *receive* them. This means you must be present with your team, listening, clarifying, challenging, inspiring, and empowering them; so that you can show them you are committed to removing obstacles for them, so that they may thrive.

Group Exercise: GROW*th* Execution

For leaders to deliver for their teams, goals must be set, but most importantly, an effective process must be followed to execute. The GROW model of coaching dates back to the United Kingdom in the 1980s, and challenges leaders to ask very specific questions. Whether you use the GROW model for your self or as a coaching mechanism, it works amazingly if you put your time and effort towards being clear, concise, and consistent. The *(annotated)* G.R.O.W model overview is as follows:

1) Goal - What is the endpoint?

2) Reality - Where are you now?

3) Obstacles/Options - What's stopping you?

4) Will - What action steps will you implement to achieve your goal?

Instructions: This exercise asks you to develop a goal statement and goal(s) that challenges you to deliver for your team. *An example goal statement is, "I want to create a psychologically safe environment for my team so that they can be more creative, innovative, and empowered to perform with excellence, without fear." An example of translating that goal statement into a goal is "My team will have more latitude and authority to make audacious business decisions."*

Next, write your Goal Statement, Goal, and answer the GROW model overview questions for your goal. *The GROW model includes several questions; for this exercise, you will only answer the four (4) provided.* Once completed, share within your small group. Afterward, share out within the larger group and discuss why you decided on the goal statement and goal that you selected.

Practical Application: Now, that you have completed this exercise, how will you introduce this model to your organization? What steps/processes will you create to ensure the GROW Model is utilized by both team leaders and their teams? What obstacles do you envision with introducing this model? How can you overcome them and challenge your team to think with a growth mindset?

ABOUT THE AUTHOR

Glenn Thomas is a North Carolina author, motivational speaker, and executive leadership facilitator who believes that every human being is inherently great. He studies leadership because he adamantly believes that leadership and life are inextricably connected. Glenn is also a doctoral student, lecturer, and community advocate. But mostly, he regards himself as a lover of life, people, and experience.

Glenn Thomas is the Founder & Managing Partner of Leadership Matters Group, a leadership development and consultancy firm with offices in Atlanta, GA, and Charlotte, NC (www.weinspirepeople.com) (www.glennathomas.com).

How to Book Glenn Thomas for professional services...

<u>Virtual & In-Person</u>
1) Executive Coaching
2) Team Learning Forums
3) Corporate Keynotes
4) Book Discussion Forums

<u>www.weinspirepeople.com</u> / <u>info@weinspirepeople.com</u>
<u>www.glennathomas.com</u> / <u>support@glennathomas.com</u>
Phone: (704) 939-8738

Heart Work: 19 Expressions of Heart-Centered Leaders...
Is the first published work written by author, motivational speaker, and executive leadership facilitator Glenn Thomas. This inspirational, thought-provoking manuscript shares Glenn's life and leadership journey, while detailing the 19 expressions of heart-centered leaders. Heart Work is filled with jewels of intra and inter-personal learning experiences, centered on the heart, mind, wellness, and leadership. This work is essential now more than ever; supporting people from all walks of life to courageously tackle matters of the heart. Heart work is in fact the most necessary work that we can undertake in our world today.

How Glenn Thomas is helping teams do their heart work...
"Heart Talks" is an exciting, transformative learning experience that focuses on three essential expressions of heart-centered leaders: extreme gratitude, intentional purpose, and resilient love. Prior to participating in this experience, the only pre-requisites are that each leader makes a personal commitment to learning, developing, and applying the attributes of heart-centered leaders in all of how they live, love and lead.

REFERENCES

1. Asghedom, E.- Ermias Joseph Asghedom (August 15, 1985 – March 31, 2019), known professionally as Nipsey Hussle (often stylized as Nipsey Hu$$le), was an American rapper, activist, and entrepreneur. https://en.wikipedia.org/wiki/Nipsey_Hussle

2. Boyz n the Hood - *Boyz n the Hood* premiered in Los Angeles on July 2, 1991, and was theatrically released in the United States ten days later. The film became a critical and commercial success, praised for its emotional weight, acting, and writing. https://en.wikipedia.org/wiki/Boyz_n_the_Hood

3. Omega Psi Phi Fraternity, Inc. - Omega Psi Phi Fraternity, Inc. is the first international fraternal organization founded on the campus of a historically black college. On the evening of November 17, 1911, Omega Psi Phi was founded inside the Science Building (later renamed Thirkield Hall) at Howard University located in Washington, D.C. The founders were three undergraduates — Edgar Amos Love, Oscar James Cooper and Frank Coleman. Joining them was their faculty adviser, Ernest Everett Just. https://oppf.org/about-omega/

4. Brown, B. (2018) "Dare to Lead" *Random House* www.brenebrown.com

5. North Carolina Central University - Founded in 1910, North Carolina Central University prepares students to succeed in the global marketplace. Consistently ranked as a top Historically Black College or University and Best Regional University in the South by U.S. News & World Report, NCCU offers flagship programs in the sciences, education, law, business, nursing and the arts. https://www.nccu.edu/we-are-nc-central

6. Orange Grove Missionary Baptist Church - Orange Grove Methodist Church—organized in a schoolhouse in 1830, by 30 members. It was located in east Durham near the Virginia-Carolina Chemical Plant. https://www.ogmbc.org/content.cfm?id=3095

7. COVID19 - Coronavirus (COVID-19) is an illness caused by a virus that can spread from person to person. The virus that causes COVID-19 is a new coronavirus that has spread throughout the world. COVID-19 symptoms can range from mild (or no symptoms) to severe illness. https://www.cdc.gov/coronavirus/2019-ncov/downloads/2019-ncov-factsheet.pdf

8. Chodron, P. (2019) "Welcoming the Unwelcome: Wholehearted Living in a Broken-hearted World" *Shambhala Publications Inc.*

9. DuVernay, A. - Winner of the Emmy, BAFTA and Peabody Awards, Academy award nominee Ava DuVernay is a writer, director, producer and film distributor. Her directorial work includes the historical drama

SELMA, the criminal justice documentary 13TH and Disney's A WRINKLE IN TIME, which made her the highest grossing black woman director in American box office history. http://www.avaduvernay.com/about

10. Farber, S. (2004) "Radical Leap" *Dearborn Trade Publishing.*
11. Sinek, S. (2014) "TED2014" https://blog.ted.com/leadership-is-about-making-others-feel-safe-simon-sinek-at-ted2014/
12. Sinek, S. (2009) "Start With Why: How Great Leaders Inspire Everyone to Take Action" *The Penguin Group.*
13. Murphy, M. (2010) "Hard Goals: The Secret to Getting from Where You Are to Where You Want to Be" *McGraw Hill.*
14. Murphy, M. (2017) "HARD Goals, Not SMART Goals, Are The Key To Career Development" https://www.forbes.com/sites/markmurphy/2017/06/11/hard-goals-not-smart-goals-are-the-key-to-career-development/#14f06dae70fb
15. Phipps, W - Wintley Phipps is a world-renowned vocal artist, education activist, motivational speaker, pastor, and CEO and Founder of the U.S. Dream Academy. https://usdreamacademy.org/staff-details.cfm?ID=18
16. Farber, S. (2020) "Love is just damn good business" *McGraw Hill* www.extremeleadership.com
17. Godfather III - The Godfather Part III is a 1990 American crime film produced and directed by Francis Ford Coppola from the screenplay co-written with Mario Puzo. It is the third and final installment in *The Godfather* trilogy. https://en.wikipedia.org/wiki/The_Godfather_Part_III
18. North Carolina A & T - North Carolina Agricultural and Technical State University advances knowledge through scholarly exchange and transforms society with exceptional teaching, learning, discovery and community engagement. An 1890 land-grant doctoral research institution with a distinction in STEM and commitment to excellence in all disciplines, North Carolina A&T creates innovative solutions that address the challenges and economic needs of North Carolina, the nation and the world. https://www.ncat.edu/about/initiatives/mission-and-vision.php
19. Lazarus, R. S., & Lazarus, B. N. (1994) "Passion and reason: Making sense of our emotions" New York: *Oxford University Press.*
20. Seppala, E. (2015) "How meditation benefits CEOs" *Harvard Business Review.*
21. Lepore, S.J., & Smyth, J. (2002) "The writing cure" Washington, DC: *American Psychological Association.*
22. Swindoll, C - Charles Rozell "Chuck" Swindoll (born October 18, 1934) is an evangelical Christian pastor, author, educator, and radio preacher. Author of "Attitude," He founded *Insight for Living*, headquartered in Frisco, Texas, which airs a radio program of the same name on more than 2,000 stations around the world in 15 languages. He is currently

senior pastor at Stonebriar Community Church, in Frisco, Texas. https://en.wikipedia.org/wiki/Chuck_Swindoll

23. Desai, P. - Panache Desai is a self-described "old friend," as shared on Oprah Winfrey's *Super Soul Sunday* television show. https://www.panachedesai.com/my-story/

24. Warren, R. - Rick Warren is an innovative pastor, renowned author, and global influencer. The various ministries Pastor Rick has created are a multi-faceted expression of his heart to bring the whole Gospel to the whole world. https://pastorrick.com

25. Thomas, E. - Eric Thomas, Ph.D. is a critically acclaimed author, World-renowned speaker, educator, pastor and audible.com Audie Awards Finalist. ET, as he is better known, has taken the world by storm, with his creative style and high-energy messages. https://etinspires.com/home

26. Tyson, C. - Cicely Tyson is an award-winning film, television and stage actress. She is notable for her roles in 'The Autobiography of Miss Jane Pittman,' 'The Help' and Broadway's 'The Trip to Bountiful,' among others. https://www.biography.com/actor/cicely-tyson

27. Capel, J. - Felton Jeffrey Capel III (born February 12, 1975) is an American college basketball coach and former player. He is currently the head coach of the University of Pittsburgh. He played for Duke University and was a head coach at Virginia Commonwealth University and University of Oklahoma. https://en.wikipedia.org/wiki/Jeff_Capel_III

28. Psalm 30:5 - https://www.bible.com/bible/111/PSA.30.5.NIV

29. Vaynerchuk, G. - Gary Vaynerchuk is the chairman of VaynerX, a modern-day media and communications holding company and the active CEO of VaynerMedia, a full-service advertising agency servicing Fortune 100 clients across the company's 4 locations. https://www.garyvaynerchuk.com/biography/

30. Angelou, M. - Dr. Maya Angelou was an American poet, memoirist, and civil rights activist. She published seven autobiographies, three books of essays, several books of poetry, and is credited with a list of plays, movies, and television shows spanning over 50 years. She received dozens of awards and more than 50 honorary degrees. https://en.wikipedia.org/wiki/Maya_Angelou

31. Gurdjian, P, Halbeisen, T, and Lane, K (2014) "Why leadership-development programs fail." *McKinsey and Company* https://www.mckinsey.com/featured-insights/leadership/why-leadership-development-programs-fail

32. Harvard Medical School (2020) "Your emotions and your heart" https://www.health.harvard.edu/heart-health/your-emotions-and-your-heart

33. Brown, T. (2008) "Thinking" *Harvard Business Review.*

34. Cowen, E.L. (1994) "The enhancement of psychological wellness: Challenges and opportunities". *American Journal of Community Psychology*, 22 (2), 149-179.

35. Ryff, C. and Keyes, C. (1995) "The Structure of Psychological Well-Being Revisited" *Journal of Personality and Social Psychology*, Vol. 69, No. 4,719-727

36. Ryan, R. M. & Deci, E. L. (2000) " Self-determination theory and the facilitation of intrinsic motivation, social development, and well-being." *American Psychologist*, pp. 55, 68-78. https://www.learning-theories.com/self-determination-theory-deci-and-ryan.html

37. https://shcs.ucdavis.edu/wellness/physical

38. (2018) "Breaking down barriers to fitness" https://www.heart.org/en/healthy-living/fitness/getting-active/breaking-down-barriers-to-fitness

39. (2017) "Depression and anxiety: Exercise eases symptoms" Mayo Clinic. https://www.mayoclinic.org/diseases-conditions/depression/in-depth/depression-and-exercise/art-20046495

40. Duncan, D. (2014) "Fitness for duty: Exercise can make you a better leader" *Forbes.*

41. (2018) "HHS Releases Physical Activity Guidelines for Americans, 2nd edition" US Department of HHS. https://www.hhs.gov/about/news/2018/11/12/hhs-releases-physical-activity-guidelines-americans-2nd-edition.html

42. The Science Behind Healthy Eating Habits. https://health.gov/our-work/food-nutrition/2015-2020-dietary-guidelines/guidelines/chapter-1/the-science-behind-healthy-eating-patterns/#eating-patterns-health

43. The National Sleep Foundation. https://www.sleepfoundation.org/articles/what-healthy-sleep

44. The National Institutes of Health. https://www.nccih.nih.gov/health/meditation-in-depth

45. (2020) "Signs of Social Wellness" University of New Hampshire. https://www.unh.edu/health/well/social-wellness

46. Kolakowski, S. (2013) "7 Signs of Emotional Wellness" *HuffPost.com*

47. (2019) "Emotional Wellness Toolkit" National Institutes of Health. https://www.nih.gov/health-information/emotional-wellness-toolkit-more-resources

48. Shah, Y. (2014) "New study proves that laughter really is the best medicine." Huff Post, https://huffpost.com/entry/laughter-and-memory n 5192086

49. Daimler, M. (2016) "Listening is an overlooked tool." Harvard Business Review, https://hbr.org/2016/05/listening-is-an-overlooked-leadership-tool

50. Greenleaf, R. - Robert Greenleaf contributed mightily to AT&T during his 38-year career there: Director of Management Development, originator of the world's first corporate assessment center, promotion of the first females and Blacks to non-menial positions, a program to expose up-and-coming leaders to the humanities, even bringing in famous theologians and psychologists to speak about the wider implications of corporate decisions. Greenleaf retired in 1964 and began his second—

and most productive—career as a writer, consultant, and teacher. https://www.greenleaf.org/about-us/robert-k-greenleaf-biography/

51. (2017) "Disengaged Employees" Gallup. https://www.gallup.com/workplace/231668/dismal-employee-engagement-sign-global-mismanagement.aspx

52. (2019) www.thesocialworkplace.com Social Workplace Organization

53. Alimo-Metcalfe, B., Alban-Metcalfe, J., Bradley, M., Mariathasan, J., and Samele, C. (2008) "The impact of engaging leadership on performance, attitudes to work and wellbeing at work: A longitudinal study." *Journal of Health Organization and Management*, Vol. 22, No. 6, pp. 586-598.

54. Dwane, A. (2016) "The 'Adaptable Leader' is the New Holy Grail - Become One, Hire One." *Management*.

55. GROW Model - The GROW model (or process) is a simple method for goal setting and problem solving. It was developed in the United Kingdom and has been used extensively in corporate coaching from the late 1980s and 1990s. https://en.wikipedia.org/wiki/GROW_model